D1431444

Act Justly

Practices to Reshape the World

Samuel Wells

CANTERBURY
PRESS
Norwich

© Samuel Wells 2022

Published in 2022 by Canterbury Press
Editorial office
3rd Floor, Invicta House,
108–114 Golden Lane,
London EC1Y OTG, UK
www.canterburypress.co.uk

Canterbury Press is an imprint of Hymns Ancient & Modern
Ltd (a registered charity)

H
Y Ancient
M
N &Modern
S

Hymns Ancient & Modern® is a registered trademark of
Hymns Ancient & Modern Ltd
13A Hellesdon Park Road, Norwich,
Norfolk NR6 5DR, UK

Scripture quotations are taken from New Revised Standard
Version Bible, Anglicized Edition, copyright © 1989, 1995
National Council of the Churches of Christ in the United States
of America. Used by permission. All rights reserved worldwide.

British Library Cataloguing in Publication data

A catalogue record for this book is available
from the British Library

ISBN 978-1-78622-457-6

Typeset by Regent Typesetting
Printed and bound in Great Britain by
CPI Group (UK) Ltd

For Steph

Contents

Preface

There are perhaps three ways to read this book. Those who want to test the mettle of the author, perhaps not having read other books from this source, may like to start by reading the Prologue and Epilogue to get a sense of my approach to perhaps the two most prominent justice issues of our day; the rest of the book will then explain how I go about putting such thoughts together. While the Prologue may appear to detach one subject from the wider conception in which it belongs, I've placed it at the beginning because in significant ways it displays the argument of the whole book. Those who want to know what I'm saying that is different from plenty of other treatments of justice may care to jump straight to the last chapter and use that as a guide to making sense of the rest; it's a perfectly legitimate way of reading the book. Others may be happy to take the book in the order in which it's presented and allow the argument to emerge, perhaps with a surprise at the end.

The book suggests how to think about justice, how to balance the justice the law addresses and the justice it does not, how to find common cause around shared goals and how, flawed as the church is, Christians may understand these common projects. I treat justice as a virtue and seek to outline what habits one may cultivate in order to become a person of justice – or, as I call it at the end of the book, a partner in justice. Accordingly, all the chapter headings are imperative verbs. The book includes many stories; indeed, as I suggest, justice is a series of conventions, each of which assumes a story. I offer several of those stories here, whose nature reflects my experience living in the USA as well as in the UK.

One distinctly countercultural thing to say in a book on this subject is that I believe the most significant initiative in seeking justice is to foster church, just as I think the most radical statement about justice is Jesus. Those are the reasons I've spent the last 30 years shaping and leading communities of faith. Not everyone sees being church as 'justice work' and it's true that many churches don't understand things that way either. But I'd like to think that the churches I've had the privilege of leading do perceive their life as an attempt to model and foster the justice of God. I don't take the view that justice and truth are alternatives or rivals. They are inseparable, and a church committed to one must be committed to the other.

The book's argument omits things some might expect to find and goes in directions some might not anticipate. For example, I don't ignore human rights, or describe them as a necessary fiction – but I don't dwell on them either. As will be clear by the end of the book, I'm not building up an account of justice from some basic theory of a social contract or an original position. Likewise, I haven't set aside several chapters to discover that there is, after all, a lot about justice in the Bible. I take that for granted. As to what might not be expected, I do suggest that investing in a system of justice, and in particular in the rule of law, is something to discuss ahead of exploring what I later call the struggle for justice. This is because upholding the institutions that advance conventional justice takes away much of the need for struggle and because struggle is in vain if it secures victories you have no way to preserve. Much depends, of course, on if you are in a state like Somalia or one more like Switzerland. I'm assuming a context more like the latter, but wanting to take time to be grateful for the exertion of those who have built the institutions that most in Somalia long for, yet many in Switzerland could easily take for granted.

I divide the argument into four parts, each with three chapters. Whereas the chapters each refer to actions that build up the virtue of justice, the parts name four distinct genres of actions. The book assumes a broad distinction between constructive justice, which aims at a legal system that functions well, and corrective justice, sometimes known as social justice, which upholds the people and causes that that system fails to serve well. So Part 2 addresses the former, while Part 3 the latter. One of my chief concerns is that passionate focus on the latter can obscure the necessary and valid attempt to pursue the former. Parts 1 and 4 envelop the argument with the beginnings and ends of justice, to which I give as much space as I do its urgent pursuit. It is in these sections, particularly in the final two chapters, that the theological concerns that underpin the enquiry emerge most fully.

Those acquainted with my extensive work on 'being with' might ask where being with sits in relation to this project. This book looks and sounds like a working-with endeavour; the constant emphasis is to avoid it lapsing into a working-for vision. But I hope the first and last chapters make clear that justice is never an end in itself but always a step on the way to something beyond: that something is being with. So *Act Justly* is in significant ways a route into being with, even though it might look

like a proclamation of working with; just as _Love Mercy_ ⚡
concerns how to restore the 'with' once it's been lost, or
how to form it if it's never been.

This book completes a trilogy that began with *Walk
Humbly* and continued with *Love Mercy*. The trilogy is
designed to be a carousel you can join at any point and
spin in either direction. *Walk Humbly* begins with the
difficulty in believing in anything; *Love Mercy* begins with
the challenge of being beset by broken relationships; *Act
Justly* begins with the reality of living in an often unfair
and frequently cruel world. The first is about faith, the
third about hope, the second about love. Each is, in its
way, an argument for the practical truth of Christianity
based on an account of how it actually works – how
it works in making meaning, how it works in reconcil-
ing the estranged, how it works in facing injustice. *Act
Justly* begs the question of how you build trust between
people, which is what *Love Mercy* is about; *Love Mercy*
begs the question of whether reconciliation truly is the
heart of all things, which is what *Walk Humbly* is about;
Walk Humbly begs the question of how one can reflect
on ultimate reality if this present reality is unbearably
unjust, which is what *Act Justly* is about; and so on.

All are rooted in the resonant words of Micah 6.8,
enquiring what the Lord requires of us – to act justly,
love mercy and walk humbly with our God. All constitute for me the fruits of a lifetime of wrestling with such
questions and seeking to live such answers as I've found.
Together they represent a desire for a holistic understanding of what it means to be a Christian: discipleship,
ministry and mission – all three; both faith and works; a
love for God, for the church and for the world; a vision
for the church and for the kingdom; worship and action;
grace and truth; justice and mercy. Such things should

never be kept apart. I would like to think that, on finishing any of the three books, a reader might exclaim, 'This is the whole gospel!' yet find themselves, on finishing another of the books, announcing, 'So is this!' – yet not disclaiming their first assertion. The argument of one presupposes and triggers the argument of the other two, in turn. In that sense, the whole project is an attempt not to put asunder what God hath joined together.

Φ

I wish it were the case that I reached all the conclusions and pursued all the arguments in this book through gentle reflection and conscientious understanding. But often I was too headstrong and prejudiced to follow such an untroubled path and it took patient and wise people, through deft persuasion and heated confrontation, to show me where I was wrong, where my experience was narrow, my heart hard and my empathy limited. For all their efforts, I still speak as a fool, and know my life has often been a poor witness to the justice I assume all who read this book seek. Nonetheless, I thank that cloud of witnesses for guiding a searcher towards truth.

Several people have helped me think through the structure of the book and the arguments it pursues. I'm grateful to Natalie Watson for asking me to give the Peckard Lecture at Peterborough Cathedral in May 2021, which gave me the chance to set out the principal lines of discussion developed here. The many threads of argument feel like the result of ongoing debates I've had with Robert Pfeiffer over countless breakfasts, lunches, coffees and walks, which I suspect he's enjoyed as much as I have. Caroline Worsfold has gently but firmly corrected my oversights and questioned my complacency for nearly 40 years and I'm grateful she's also refined the ideas detailed here. I'm indebted to Chris Braganza and Frances Stratton for offering very helpful perspectives on law that greatly enriched Chapters 4 and 5. I've explored the urgency and intractability of these questions with Stanley Hauerwas for 30 years, and I trust will do so for many more; my gratitude to him will never be done. I appreciate the honesty, example, thoughtfulness and insight of other kind readers – Farley Lord, Anna Poulson, Ruth Taunt and Maureen Knudsen Langdoc – each of whom has shown me what I've left out, worded poorly or misunderstood. I'm thankful too for Christine Smith, who helped me conceive the trilogy and bring it to publication.

The book is dedicated to my daughter Stephanie, with two petitions that are also laments: that her generation makes steps to resolve some of the pressing issues of justice that my own generation has so culpably bequeathed to it; and that, in her lifetime, church becomes synonymous with justice, and justice with church, in a way too seldom experienced today.

Prologue: Racial Justice

I recall being on the terraces at the Easter Road stadium in Edinburgh in 1988 watching Hibernian play Rangers. This was before the Hillsborough disaster, so we were all standing. Mark Walters was the first Black player in the Scottish league for a generation, and he was on the wing for Rangers. Every time he came to the corner beneath where I was standing, two men near me started monkey chanting. I had no idea what to do. I was too cowardly to confront them. I felt sick and wanted to move away. I wondered how Mark Walters would react, if he was used to it, if it made it impossible to play. I felt part of something horrible. That combination of horror, shame, anger and powerlessness is one that recurs often when the reality of racism is painfully revealed.

But for those who are its target, it can prove deadly. In August 2021 in Liverpool, Zakiya Janny watched as her attacker was sentenced to eight years for slashing her face with a machete as she protected her four-year-old son in a local park. Her attacker left a five-inch wound. The vile epithets he shouted as he assaulted her made it clear he had no motive other than racial hatred. The line between such vicious violence and the chants directed at Mark Walters is clear and unambiguous. And yet, as I stood on the terraces in my early twenties, I was only beginning to wake up to how the culture I'd grown up in

was saturated with racist assumptions, jokes and judgements, systems and structures; how I'd participated
in all these things, as if they were the air I breathed;
and how they were intrinsically linked to subjugation,
violence and death.

There's no question that the urgency of the conversation about race picked up after May 2020, as the
George Floyd murder demonstrated that racism is a
deadly reality today, not a gruesome inheritance from
history. I want to acknowledge three reasons why race
is a challenging topic. First, almost every term and argument in this conversation is contested and contextual. To
take an example, the phrase 'person of colour' is today
a positive assertion of identity; but the term 'coloured
person' is frowned upon. That's about context. But even
that statement is contested. So nothing I say here is free
of controversy.

Second, a person who looks and talks like me may
not be the right person to lead this conversation. That's
because the assumption that, whatever the problem is,
it's for the white guy to define it, fix it and take the credit
for it, is central to what we're talking about. Scrambling
such tendencies is essential to imagining a better future.
It's called decentring – ceasing to think that the white
guy is the centre of the story and carefully reshaping
imagination and society accordingly. Whether that can
be advanced by a white guy writing a book I'll let you
judge when you've finished reading it. I've written the
book because I'm hoping to establish how a person from
my location can take responsibility for seeking justice
without thereby becoming the centre of the conversation.

Put my second challenge together with my first, and
you have a third: the word 'we'. Often a writer will
speak of 'we' as if the whole readership and anyone else

engaged constitute a single body with a united view of the world. But on this issue, that's just not true. Some people live with limited opportunities, significant risk of verbal or physical assault and widespread discrimination, while others don't. And there's a lingering, if often false, assumption that a book is where the author gets to tell the world what it should do – and that whole idea breaks down because what we each need to do depends on our social location.

Having recognized the dangers of any writing on this subject reinforcing precisely the things that need to be dismantled, I want to separate out the different things we're talking about when we talk about race, particularly in the UK. I suggest that at the bottom of the evil of racism is the sin that leads humans, in their anxiety about deprivation and death, to attempt to make themselves secure, superior and sacred, and as part of that, to create hierarchies that control other humans and treat some as of lesser value. Such oppression inevitably creates antagonism. To offset the guilt of what is done and to defuse the retribution anticipated, oppressors then create a whole ideology that justifies the subjugation such action has brought about. Once that process has been going on for centuries, it becomes hard for everyone, persecutor or persecuted, to think outside the habits and language it involves. Then, when a construct has emerged, it can be manipulated in such a way that those subject to it come to be blamed for precisely the situation that was deliberately created to keep them subservient.

Beyond those general characteristics, racism in the Black Lives Matter era has focused particularly on the legacy of slavery and segregation in the USA, and how to be an African American today is to be liable to state-sanctioned violence, incarceration and murder, constituting a society-wide declaration that Black lives don't matter. While Britain ended slavery much earlier than the USA, it remained, through the Mississippi-Manhattan-Manchester cotton production triangle, a central part of the slave economy. Racism is about economics before it becomes about prejudice.

But there are differences between Britain and the USA. African Americans are 400-year residents who can trace their ancestors on American soil further back than the great majority of other Americans. While there have always been Black people in Britain, the presence of large numbers is largely a post-war phenomenon. Many Black Britons trace ancestry to the Caribbean and often know what it means to share their surname with that of the man who owned their forebears' bodies. But more trace heritage to Africa and have no direct ancestral legacy of slavery. Meanwhile, those from the Indian subcontinent and elsewhere experience racism but are outside the Atlantic slave story entirely. The overarching story of empire that unites the Indian subcontinent, Africa and the Caribbean affirms that race and economics have long been inseparable. It doesn't for a moment mean that racism in the UK is not real, sinister and a scar on church and society. It just means we can't take a US template and transfer it straightforwardly to the UK like a Broadway production coming to the West End.

The central paradox of talking about racism is this. On the one hand, racism is a construct. It's not biologically defensible. Any notion that races are clearly distinguishable, that one is superior to another or that they're inherently at odds with each other, is nonsense. If you go back far enough, we're all related to each other. Race is not a fundamental human characteristic. On the other hand, race is everywhere: it's invoked as a battle for power, purity, identity, justice. To discount or try to ignore race is naïve, idealistic and too often part of a sinister agenda.

The world is not racial, in that significant differences are in our DNA; but it's certainly racialized, such that we can't simply relate to one another as if race is irrelevant to how we experience life. As Ibram X. Kendi puts it, 'It is one of the ironies of antiracism that we must identify racially in order to identify the racial privileges and dangers of being in our bodies.'[1] Racism is a poison that's not inherent in the world, not natural in the world, but is at large in the world. This is the paradox we perpetually reckon with: this venom that shouldn't be in the world but nonetheless characterizes so much of the world. We must never underestimate its pervasiveness and power, but we must never regard it as basic to humanity or creation.

Once we've expressed the issue that way, it becomes a little less overwhelming to explore what we should do about it. I suggest we need to pursue two approaches simultaneously: one based on addressing present racism and the legacies of oppression all around us; the other about imagining, practising and inhabiting a different world.

As to present racism, for society, while racism is damaging in any circumstance, it becomes destructive when combined with political and economic (and not just social) power. Pursuing racial equality without addressing social inequality is only half a policy; seeking economic equality without addressing racial inequality is just as flawed. Plenty of people have faced racial

---

1 Ibram X. Kendi, *How to be an Antiracist* (London: The Bodley Head, 2019), p. 38.

discrimination and yet found paths to flourishing; but when you add social and economic disadvantage, you've got an even greater mountain to climb. Government can't abolish racism, but it can address economic and social barriers that amplify the damage racism does. It can also avoid divisive rhetoric that sets those against each other on racial grounds whose interests would otherwise coincide.

As to imagining differently, the church needs a radical transformation in its understanding of who God is. God is no different from the face we see in Jesus, and Jesus is not a north European white male: he is a Middle Eastern member of an oppressed race in an occupied country, born homeless, killed because his people were not protected by the rule of law, and then, in a common racial move, blamed for his own oppression. If an artist portrays a Black Jesus on the cross, it's still considered provocative – but it's closer to history than a white one. The risen and ascended Jesus asks St Paul on the road to Damascus, 'Why are you persecuting me?' The Christ made present in the Holy Spirit poses the same question to racists today.

Moving to the second approach to racism, inhabiting a different world, I want to highlight the words, 'You are a chosen race, a royal priesthood, a holy nation, God's own people.' It's a commonplace, often attributed to Rosa Parks, that, 'There's only one race, the human race.' Biologically that's true, but 1 Peter makes the bold claim that in baptism, Christians become part of a new race. In contrast to the distorted modern conception of race, the scriptural notion of race begins in Exodus 19, where God proclaims the Jews 'a priestly kingdom and a holy nation'. In 1 Peter 2, race is transformed from a genetic category conferred at conception to a gift bestowed on anyone who finds their home in God. Race is about God's claiming of each one of us, not our identifying ourselves or others. Race is something none of us have, all can be given, and none can lose. In baptism, we join a new race. The so-called race we were born into is sociologically significant. But our primary identity is thenceforth the one we receive.

The gospel's prescription for a society beyond racist injustice and racialized identities is for us to discover what it means for our identities to be gifts from God that we cherish in each other and ourselves. Identity is not something imposed by others that is feared or despised. It's not even something we craft by ourselves that is clung to and defended. It's a gift from God. Holiness is not a mythical purity or isolated superiority but a truly engaged gentleness and gracious encounter. Priesthood is not a role played by a few to save or lord it over others, but a gift to all to remind us who we are and to draw out the diverse gifts God has given each one of us.

That society beyond racism, that priestly kingdom and holy nation, is what 1 Peter calls church. The sad truth is that the church has peddled false ideologies of racialized injustice at least as much as anyone else, and even when it has found a better vision, it has frequently failed to realize that vision. But by describing the church as a race, 1 Peter shows that racism isn't an unfortunate human shortcoming or an inevitable struggle to comprehend difference: it's blasphemy – the failure to perceive God's true nature and purpose – and idolatry – the attempt to impose a false form of salvation, in this case by the ostracism and oppression of others. Thus, cherishing the diverse gifts of one another isn't just ethics, the ordering of our life in the image of God – it's actually worship, our very recognition of and response to God.

If we can't reflect in our lives the gift of becoming a new race together, we're not simply a sinful church: we're not really a church at all.

My mind goes back to Mark Walters. How does he, on the football field, play on when beset by hostility, ridicule and abuse? And how do I, in the stands, find ways to challenge those whose chanting expresses hatred and threats of violence? Since Mark Walters retired, he's spent his life organizing to eliminate racism from football. It's for each of us, in our own spheres of life, to organize and do the same.

PART I

Perceiving Justice

Is there such a thing as justice in itself, or does the term 'justice' name a collection of always-incomplete strategies for addressing injustice? I suggest there is such a thing as justice. But before pursuing it, or seeking to counter injustice, we need to explore three things. First, where justice fits into our moral imagination – what is it an alternative to, what are the things closely related to it or easily mistaken for it. Second, how we put that imagination to work by being trained to see and to listen and be alert to where things are wrong and need to be put right. Third, to what extent we are up to our necks in the things we are denouncing – and thus how we avoid both the passivity of feeling we can never get it right and the self-righteousness of turning the world into a version of ourselves. These are, I suggest, the three preliminaries to engaging with justice. They thus form the subject of my first three chapters.

PART 1

Learning Jersey

I

Imagine

Human beings are made not simply to live, but to be fully alive; not merely to exist, but to flourish. Plenty of things inhibit human beings from flourishing. Some of those hindrances are constraints of existence in general – advancing age, faltering faculties, bodily fragility, unfortunate circumstances; we could call these, which are not necessarily bad things in themselves, contingency. Some are the fruits of limited options or the unintended results of unwise choices – the commitment hastily entered into, the reckless mistake, the self-destructive impulse; we could call these folly. But others stem from neither bad luck nor bad judgement. They come from our misuse at the hands of one another. The denial of a child's opportunity for education and a start in life, the exclusion of a person on account of an aspect of their identity deemed unworthy or threatening, the seizing of what rightly belonged to an individual by a person who thought they could take it without redress; these we call injustice.

No one is immune to contingency and folly. Contingency is notoriously unevenly distributed, though it catches up with everyone in the end. Folly is part of every life, however hard many try to excise it by earnest discipline or mitigate its consequences by the manipulation of power. But many people, perhaps most, globally, find their path to flourishing thwarted chiefly by injust-ice. In some instances, this refers to an egregious wrong perpetrated against them as an individual – a crime that shattered an emerging dream or sliced off a plant before it flowered. But more often, a person experiences injustice along with a host of others, because a whole group is oppressed, subjugated or trodden down in a subtle or systematic programme orchestrated to favour one kind of person over another.

Because such patterns are so widespread; because they can, in so many instances, be imposed from an early age, if not birth; and because they exchange the glorious gift of difference known as diversity for a perceived differ-ence that becomes the pretext for indignity, the quest to overturn injustice can flood the imagination of anyone who equates the good with the flourishing of all. And so, perhaps, it should. But a passionate desire to remove something has to be accompanied by an equal commit-ment to put something else in its place. Liberation lies not just in shaking off chains but in genuine flourishing. The task of articulating what flourishing entails does not indicate resistance to the urgency of fighting injustice. It could, on the contrary, constitute the most necessary complement to fighting injustice: practising justice. The practice of any pursuit begins in the imagination – for before you can bring something about, you have to have some notion of what it is you are seeking to create. When you're fighting against the bad, it's easy to lose sight of what the good might look like.

So before exploring what it means to act against injust-ice, we need to begin by imagining justice. Whenever we're horrified or incensed by what we regard as an act of injustice, we're assuming that there's something called justice, which isn't entirely out of reach and does exist somewhere, to be restored, imitated or at least approximated. To summon up such a vision of justice is an act of the imagination. It goes beyond a society in which laws are passed, kept and enforced, to a truly harmonious world of peace and flourishing. It is the full flowering of the virtue of hope.

Here are two contrasting portrayals. In his 2002 novel *Family Matters*, Rohinton Mistry describes the intense and multi-layered life of Mumbai. One of his characters, Vikram, describes it as a city that 'endures because it gives and receives ... the spirit of tolerance, acceptance, generosity'. He describes seeing a train leaving the platform, completely packed. Everyone had given up chasing it. Except one. 'Suddenly, he raised his arms. And people on the train reached out and grabbed them.' Vikram feared for the man's life.

> A moment later, they had lifted him off the platform. Now his feet were dangling outside the compartment, and I almost screamed to stop the train. His feet pedalled in the air ... There he was, hanging, his life literally in the hands of strangers. And he had put it there. He had trusted them. More arms reached out and held him tight in their embrace. It was a miracle – suddenly he was completely safe.

Then Vikram realized that what he'd seen was not a miracle. 'It happened over and over: hands reaching out to help, as though it were completely normal, a routine commuter procedure.'[1]

---

1 Rohinton Mistry, *Family Matters* (London: Faber & Faber, 2002), pp. 159–60.

Mistry's novel contrasts two views of the city – one, like this, a perpetual miracle, the other, contested, full of animosity, deceit and violence. Vikram's vision is one of true justice, where selfless people working seamlessly and unbidden in true partnership bring life out of death and reward trust with collaboration and kindness. As Vikram says, 'Anywhere else in the world, in those so-called civilised places like England and America',[2] that collective spirit would never be found and people would never find such common cause.

Meanwhile, in his 2019 novel *This is Happiness*, Niall Williams describes the village of Faha in the west of Ireland in 1958, as the 17-year-old Noe sojourns there following his mother's death. Staying with his grandparents, and sharing a room with the itinerant electrical engineer Christy, Noe experiences the breadth and depth of a culture about to be transformed by the coming of electricity. Every dimension of local life is portrayed, from waiting in line for a letter at the post office, to the chemist's shop with its uneven linoleum, to the encyclopaedia salesman offering limitless wisdom, to the ruminating cows, 'made slow-witted by the rain'.[3] Yet there is honest dealing too, and echoes of love, from the continuous feud between Noe's grandparents to Christy's lifelong passion for the woman he deserted to Noe's own longings for each of the widowed doctor's three daughters. This is not a book about a struggle for justice, but about kindness, forbearance and stories that 'must never arrive at a point, or risk conclusion'. It's not without grief or mistakes – contingency and folly are all around – but it's short on malice. Lest a description

---

2 Mistry, *Family Matters*, p. 159.

3 Niall Williams, *This is Happiness* (London: Bloomsbury, 2019).

of justice become abstract, this novel offers a picture of what a healthy, flourishing community looks like without superlative achievement or the admirable overcoming of adversity.

What are the characteristics of such a community? Faha has no great distinctions between the wealthy and the poor. The doctor's beautiful daughters have a level of aspiration beyond most of the local children, but they have no inherited wealth or extensive social connections to lift them way beyond the common lot; they go to the same cinema and fraternize with the same schoolmates as everyone else. There's equality of opportunity: Noe's companion Christy has gone in search of a fortune; his one-time beloved, the chemist's widow, has found her way locally. Neither is regarded as the better path. There's a real sense of agency: few, if any, feel their lives don't matter – because they have an honoured role in their community and they can make life better for themselves and others. The arrival of electricity is a curiosity, not the supply of needed resources to a people perpetually in deficit. Most of all, there's a sense of genuine belonging, where each is respected and cherished, regardless of intellectual achievement or social standing. These are not sentimental things: they are the embodiment of what justice looks like.[4]

Let me paint three spheres in which we might imagine justice. One is the ideal; the second is striving for the ideal; the third is a realistic condition one might settle for – a deal.

---

4 Ferdinand Mount, 'Five types of inequality', *Joseph Rowntree Foundation*, 10 December 2007, https://www.jrf.org.uk/report/five-types-inequality provides a helpful contemporary analysis of the relationship of justice and equality that has shaped my understanding of Faha here.

The Christian word for the vision of true justice is heaven. Christians have no monopoly on such an aspiration. The Marxist anticipation of a withering-away of the state, yielding a genuine communist economy, is an ideal – one that disdains any consideration of a transcendent realm, but a vision of justice, nonetheless; a version of heaven. For Christians, heaven has a number of distinctive characteristics. It is fundamentally being in full and uninhibited relationship with God. This is conventionally called worship, but worship merely means the according of due dignity and value to God. Right relationship means more than that. It means a due proportion of awe and intimacy, where the increase of the one only amplifies the other and where the overflowing trust and community of the Trinity is extended to embrace humanity also. On that combination of honour and joy rests the restoration of the three other key relationships. There is a transformation of relationship with one another, in which there is a corresponding balance of respect and reverence, enjoyment of difference and delight in complementarity. There is the consummation of creation, in which violence, rivalry and privation give way to effervescent abundance and rewarding companionship. And there is an ultimate reconciliation with oneself, as the restless heart finds its rest in God. All these mercies are embodied in the person of Christ: for Christ is humanity standing fully before God and God standing fully before humanity and the two rejoicing in one another. Christ is the neighbour fully embraced; Christ is the fullness of creation upheld and restored – resurrected – before God; and Christ is the reconciliation of each of our selves. This is what it means to say Christ is all in all.

But we are not, currently, in heaven. We are either

striving for an ideal or settling for a deal. The name Christians give to striving for the ideal is church. Again, Christians have no monopoly on striving for an ideal. There are some who hold the United States' Constitution in such high regard that they believe all that needs to be done on any issue is to interpret that constitution correctly and justice will be served. There are those who drafted and seek to recraft the Universal Declaration on Human Rights in the same spirit. There are others for whom a political party or a form of broad-based organizing is a 'church' – a community in which all are together, harnessing each other's gifts, addressing common obstacles and striving for an ideal. But for Christians, church is the embodiment of Christ and anticipation of heaven, the place where, through the Holy Spirit, the full humanity of Christ and the full divinity of Christ continue to meet. It is not a denial that the Holy Spirit also works elsewhere – that Christ plays in 10,000 places – but it is a conviction that in the word of Scripture and sermon, the practice of prayer and devotion, the encounter of sacrament and service, Christ is made flesh among us, and we can trust that God is at work. Church is not heaven: it is not the eradication of contingency, folly or injustice; but it is the conscious and intentional collective striving for the ideal – of justice, but also of mercy, of truth and of love. There is no hope in heaven; it is not needed, for all is fulfilled; hope is instead the church's characteristic virtue in this time of contingency, folly and injustice.

Then, third, there is settling for a deal. This is loosely called world. Again, Christians are not alone in having a notion of an imperfect milieu that is far from ideal. 'That's the way the world is', says almost every parent to almost every disillusioned child, on the first occasion cruelty, discrimination or unfairness intrude into their well-being. For Christians, 'world' has a particular meaning. World is that which has taken the freedom of God's patience not yet to believe. Christianity perceives a story by which there is creation, there is the calling of Abraham and his descendants as God's people, there is the coming of Christ, and there will be the last day. Secularity, or 'world', has no such story: there is simply a sequence of events. There is no sacred shape to those events. World is characterized by deals that make the unsatisfactory tolerable, the inadequate manageable, the incomplete sustainable. Sometimes – often, perhaps usually and normally – the ideal is so far out of sight that even striving for it is rare and seems fanciful.

But that doesn't mean world is simply a negative thing. Just as church is not heaven, but is shot through with contingency, folly and injustice, despite best efforts to withstand them, especially the latter two, so world is laced with examples of grace and epiphanies of glory, not only in the wider creation, but among people too. The Spirit makes elements of heaven visible in church and world, often beyond the explicit agency of the church. The name for this is kingdom. By the agency of the Holy Spirit, kingdom breaks into the flawed life of the church and the compromised life of the world. Such moments can be described as living God's future now.

These descriptions help us perceive where justice fits in. Just as peace is not simply that which begins when the last gun stops firing, but a concrete set of interactions and blessings, so justice is not simply the overthrow of injustice, but the embodiment of healthy and fruitful relationships of mutual upbuilding and common flourishing. Justice names the highest aspiration the church has for the world, short of the world becoming the church.

Justice isn't the same as kingdom, because kingdom names something infused by the Holy Spirit, whereas justice is something humanity can appropriately aspire to for itself. Justice, in the sense of a peaceable vision of well-being and thriving, is invariably out of reach; but it's always within sight, in the sense that its constituent qualities can always be identified and worked towards. Justice also names the least expectation the world can have of the church, given that the church's striving goes beyond justice to truth and love – but should never fall below the standard of justice. Justice is, to a large degree, the tangible form love takes, beyond a personal circle of relationships, in a world beset by contingency and folly.

Justice means everyone has a chance to flourish; love means walking alongside a person so they find every encouragement to take that chance. Justice requires that everyone has access to opportunity, education, training, apprenticeship, formation; love requires accompanying a person so that they turn those possibilities into full realities. Justice entails that no one is forced into a life-direction against their will; love entails supporting a person as they use their freedom well. Justice is thus the absolutely necessary, but invariably insufficient, con-stituent of flourishing life for individuals, groups and communities. It cannot guarantee flourishing – but it can ensure that arbitrary and inexcusable obstacles to flourishing are dismantled. It cannot provide fairness in the face of contingency or second chances in the wake of folly – but it can promise vindication and rectification in the face of malicious sabotage or unwarranted exploitation.

Christians seek justice because church and kingdom are the two ways in which they anticipate the life of for ever today, and justice is a foundational condition of the life of for ever. Seeking justice is the way Christians work to make the world the best it can be and meanwhile to minimize the damage of the dysfunctions of the church. To seek justice is not to dictate what flourishing looks like, but to create and renew the conditions by which all people might flourish in their own way.

Lurking in the shadows of the pursuit of justice is the unavoidable – but unfashionable – question of judgement.[5] The concept of judgement requires reappraisal. That's because judgement is often characterized as the inappropriate imposition of prejudice – a prejudice that forms a negative estimation of a person, when in truth that person deserves much better – and an imposition that diminishes the person in their own eyes and the eyes of others; in other words, itself a form of injustice. But such a characterization requires expansion. There is a positive understanding of judgement. Judgement is a truthful evaluation of circumstances and character that perceives real motives and genuine outcomes, such that no harmful action or damaging cruelty goes unnoticed or unaddressed but is brought to light and seen for what it is. Thus, judgement becomes not only understandable or inevitable, but good, essential and vital, because it ultimately means the vindication of the oppressed. The good news of Christianity is not that there's no judgement. That wouldn't be good news, because it would mean the oppressed would languish in subjection and wrongdoers would walk unchallenged, free to inflict harm elsewhere. Instead, the good news is that judgement does not have the last word.

---

5 The definitive treatment of justice as judgement is Oliver O'Donovan, *The Ways of Judgment: The Bampton Lectures, 2003* (Grand Rapids, MI: Eerdmans, 2005).

Only after the issuing of judgement can there be mercy. To exercise mercy doesn't mean not to judge – it means using the power that judgement gives you not to destroy the one judged, but to transform, rehabilitate and repair them. Beyond judgement there is never simply destruction: for the victim there is, eventually, restoration, while for the oppressor there is, sooner or later, some form of mercy. Mercy never means bypassing or abolishing judgement; it means that any punishment is motivated and modified by the desire not to wreak vengeance but ultimately to heal. There is a name for the final restoration of victims and rehabilitation of offenders: that name is resurrection. The reason justice is central for Christians is because it is an indispensable stepping stone on the road to resurrection.

But reticence in regard to the language and necessity of judgement discloses an irony that underlies the Christian pursuit of justice. Traditional Christianity understands that, in the face of judgement, all have been found wanting. And if justice were truly served, all would stand condemned. The crucifixion of Jesus only begins to make sense if one ceases to blame the throng in Jerusalem around Passover for his death and recognizes that we are all to blame. We are to blame because we are each party to the envy, small-mindedness, pride, selfishness, duplicity, cowardice, laziness and vindictiveness that brought Christ's execution about. And for each of us, those unworthy attitudes and actions are signs of grotesque ingratitude for the gifts of life and care to which we owe our existence. So the irony is that Christianity is founded on an enormous injustice – the injustice that none of us have to bear the final cost of our malice and folly. The conventional adage that justice means giving to each their due would leave all, eternally, in a sorry state. It is therefore less from righteous indignation, or passionate virtue, that Christians seek justice: it is out of humble gratitude for the gift of existence and heart-felt wonder at the gift of God's mercy by which we do not ultimately bear the cost of having treated that gift so poorly. Justice begins in the imagination – and the Christian imagination is one set on fire by the miracle of grace.

2

See

Justice begins with the imagination. Addressing injustice begins with perception. You have to see it before you do anything about it. Once your imagination has been trained in the ways of the ideal, striving for that ideal, and making a deal, your gaze is ready to recognize what is none of those things – to see what should not be. An imagination infused by grace yields a perception that becomes used to distinguishing between contingency, folly and injustice. Rather than say the surrendered, 'It's all too complicated', or the sweeping, 'People earn their own luck', or even the fatalistic, 'What goes round, comes round', an imagination set on fire by grace makes more careful judgements. Contingency elicits compassion; folly requires understanding; injustice, once seen and perceived, demands response. With these trained perceptions, you are ready to discern the subtleties of what is taking place before you.

Let's imagine you're looking for a cheap place to get your car washed. You land on a site near a local park. You drive in and encounter a man who speaks your language well. The price is good. The man encourages you to leave your keys, get a coffee nearby and return in half an hour. But, two minutes later, you realize you left your phone in the car. So you return before getting a coffee. You see a dozen males, some of them under

16, being spoken to harshly, and in one case being physically coerced. You sense the men are exhausted. The ones who are not yet men look vulnerable and withdraw when they see you. When you notify the police, it turns out the employer holds all the men's passports, houses them in two substandard and overcrowded caravans and frequently subjects them to intimidation and verbal abuse. You thought you were getting a cheap car wash. It turns out you were colluding in modern slavery.

Reflecting on what you saw, you realize hundreds of people have had their cars washed before you and said nothing. Why? Perhaps because they'd seen nothing – as you would have done, had you not gone back for your phone. Or perhaps they'd seen what you'd seen, but not perceived what it truly was. Maybe they had no notion of an ideal, or striving for an ideal. Maybe in their world of deals, the deal they saw in front of them didn't seem so unusual or make them uneasy. Injustice proliferates because people don't see – because they look away, choose not to see, don't perceive the truth of what they're seeing, or are deceived.

Injustice is seldom as straightforward as such a case of modern slavery. More often, injustice operates on several levels. The Swedish film *The Girl with the Dragon Tattoo*, and its two sequels *The Girl Who Played with Fire* and *The Girl Who Kicked the Hornet's Nest*, tell the story of Lisbeth Salander. Lisbeth is a young woman who has experienced a chaotic childhood with a violent father. She has witnessed and been subject to things no child should know. Escaping torture, and at the same time seeking to protect her mother, Lisbeth tried, when a child, to kill her father. Yet rather than discover what made her do so, the authorities blame her and subsequently seek to protect the world from her. Having failed to kill her father, she's placed under guardianship that continues into adulthood. Meanwhile, she pursues an unorthodox career of hacking and covert surveillance.

Her long-standing guardian retires, and she's deprived of the single constant and reliable presence in her life. To compound this, her new guardian turns out to be not a friend but an enemy. Holding almost complete control over her life, from the outset he demands, as the price of his not submitting a condemnatory report about her, to be at liberty to assault her sexually on demand. Yet he underestimates Lisbeth. She turns out to be no powerless victim. In a scene that blends trauma and revenge, she apparently yields to his attack, only for it to transpire that she's filmed the whole episode. She turns the tables on him, incapacitating him with a taser and strapping him down. She proceeds to tattoo on his chest words that name precisely what kind of a man he is.

Later, it transpires that Lisbeth's guardian is part of a ring of influential people in Stockholm involved in human trafficking and exploitation. It also comes to light that Lisbeth's father was a grand-scale criminal in Russia who's been protected in Sweden because he's been providing classified information to the West; hence the authorities' reluctance to prosecute him when Lisbeth was a child. Because of a second attempt to kill her father, again out of self-protection, Lisbeth has to stand trial. Her guardian continues to use his power over her liberty and finances to silence her and seek to engineer a guilty verdict. For the second time, Lisbeth has to face the ghastly truth about her childhood and about her guardian, and on this occasion she has to lay those details bare in open court. In a way that only happens in the movies, all the plot lines converge at the end of the third film: Lisbeth's guardian is caught out not only by her, when she shows the video of her assault to an aghast court, but by journalists, and lastly by the police, as the facts about the human trafficking ring finally come to light.

The story vividly portrays four dimensions of injustice. The first is the wilful mistreatment Lisbeth suffers at the hands of her father, an injustice that continues to threaten her as long as he remains alive, and whose effects are palpably permanent. This is a crime committed by one person against another that requires, at the very least, arrest, prosecution, conviction and punishment; none of which ever happen. The second dimension is the way Lisbeth's guardian manipulates her for his own sordid gratification. This is different from the first case of injustice because it involves professional misconduct. It's difficult to believe that such a person has left it until late in his career to perpetrate such exploitation – almost certainly his behaviour has been overlooked or condoned by others who were to some degree aware of his grotesque misdemeanours. Thus, it's an injustice rooted in institutional failure: the fostering of a culture of oppression. The third level of injustice in the story is the human trafficking ring: this is a corporate criminal project involving middle agents, abduction, imprisonment and enslavement. It's an underworld stretching beyond Sweden, doubtless drawing in multiple authorities who, by failing to do their job, permit the proliferation of modern slavery. The fourth dimension is the discovery that Lisbeth's father has been shielded by the Swedish government itself, with the knowledge of those in the highest offices of state, in collaboration with the leaders and intelligence agencies of the most powerful countries of the West. This is damaging in a different way from the other dimensions of injustice: here the country's leaders, charged with ensuring justice, are complicit in perpetuating injustice, revealing corruption at every level of society – but justifying it because it promises to give the West some strategic advantage over Russia. At this point the viewer's whole impulse to separate right from wrong is brought into question, and at one stage in the story it becomes difficult to establish who is implicated and who is not: trust is completely undermined.

The injunction to see directs our attention not just to surface levels of injustice, like Lisbeth's treatment by her father and guardian, but the more complex hinterland of injustice that often lies behind it. Often the impulse is to intervene, or assume someone else should: but in such a case as this, any intervention may exacerbate injustices elsewhere. By stretching the drama over three films, this narrative makes clear how complex and interwoven the issues are. Addressing injustice is often no simple thing.

Seeing must include listening. Acting justly isn't first of all about what you say but about who you listen to. Lisbeth isn't listened to as a child; no one seems to have asked why she tried to kill her father; no one is interested in what it's like to be at the mercy of a ruthless and predatory guardian; no one seems much bothered about listening to her even at her trial, until she produces the video that turns the tables on her guardian. Sometimes even when you can't see, you can still listen: seeing assumes the primary agency is yours; listening shifts that agency to the one who is telling you their story. Seeing is notoriously subject to misunderstanding or misreading; listening is a way of letting the person in pain shape the narrative, beginning where they want to begin, and describing for themselves what justice might look like.

The philosopher Paul Ricœur, when speaking of interpreting texts, especially the Bible, coins the term 'the second naïveté'.[1] He means that when we read the Bible as a child, we take the stories at face value. When we read them as an adult, we do so with eyes trained in scientific, psychological and emotional scepticism. But to read the stories appropriately, we need to suspend that scepticism temporarily and read them in a way that allows them to transform us. We could employ a similar approach with, for example, critical race theory. Critical race theory rejects the simplistic and self-serving assumption that racism is due to and located in the straightforward prejudices of individuals. Instead, it highlights how racism arises within complex social and institutional dynamics that can operate independently of any one individual's active complicity. It becomes embedded in manners, habits and mores that mean it is less often an explicit and intended slight and more often an unconscious and apparently benign word or action. Equipped with this perspective, and schooled by innumerable examples, a person seeking justice has lost any naïveté they may once have had. But to see injustice may require adopting a second naïveté. It may begin with simple observations that defy individualized explanations: 'I wonder why only people of one race have applied for this job.' 'I wonder why, when the teacher asks for ideas from the class, five of the students are never the first to speak.' 'I wonder why, when this government scheme was launched, only people of one race tended to take it up.' 'I wonder why, when we talk about "people of colour", white people are assumed to be normal, and not to have something we call colour.' In Hans Christian Andersen's 1837 folktale 'The Emperor's New Clothes', the emperor walks

---

1 Paul Ricœur, *The Symbolism of Evil*, translated by Emerson Buchanan (New York: Harper & Row, 1967), pp. 232–78, 306–46.

naked through the city, and all his subjects admire him, until a child says he is wearing nothing. Racism can so grip the imagination of all parties, including sometimes its victims, that it sometimes takes a straightforward, apparently naïve observation to break the spell.

Seeing injustice is thus often greatly helped by education in the subtleties, sophistication and sinister extent of nefarious social demarcation. But it's seldom a simple matter of pointing the finger at an egregious crime perpetrated in broad daylight. The schooling that's required certainly involves understanding a whole range of challenging and revealing study, research and insight. Yet often the question goes back to the one raised in the previous chapter: these people may not be living an ideal, or even striving for an ideal – but why have they settled for such a poor deal? Was someone coerced into this deal, so it was never truly a deal at all – or has this deal been so surreptitiously constructed and invisibly framed that even most of its beneficiaries would deny it was either a bad deal or a deal at all – just the way of things? So then the question is, if this is so far from ideal, why would anyone make such a deal? How on earth have things come to the point that this is considered the way of the world? Who are the beneficiaries of this arrangement, and who is going to set up obstacles in the way of bringing about change?

And there you see the people who at best collude in, and at worst orchestrate, injustice.

To give another example, you see forms of protest. There could be a march. There could be violent clashes. There may be a boycott of stores, or goods. What do you see? Do people do these things for fun? Are all such events a cover for criminal looting, taking revenge on personal antagonists and the venting of an anarchist urge for destruction? Maybe they are, in a small minority of cases. Far more often, it's a boiling-over of tension, a desperate expression of hurt, an outlet for years of frustration, a sign that the 'deal' is hopelessly biased against those demonstrating pain and exclusion. To see injustice is to ask, 'Why are these people doing damage to their own community?' If it were criminal activity, surely they would pillage elsewhere. Who or what is the focus of their anger? The simple adage 'no smoke without fire' leads an observer back through the story to seek to understand who lit the fire. And who is actually burning.

In Maggie O'Farrell's 2006 novel, *The Vanishing Act of Esme Lennox*, Iris Lockhart receives a phone call from a mental hospital, which is about to close down and must rehouse all its residents.[2] Iris learns that she has a great aunt, Esme, sister to Iris' grandmother – a grandmother who had always maintained she was an only child. Wary of the responsibility of taking on an unpredictable elderly relative, Iris' curiosity nonetheless leads her to discover the truth about Esme. Her mysterious great aunt experienced a difficult childhood in colonial India followed by teenage years in censorious Edinburgh. Iris needs courage, compassion and perseverance to see what otherwise could scarcely be believed: in the 1930s, all it took for a father or a husband to commit a rebellious – or pregnant – woman to an asylum for life was a GP's signature. Esme isn't insane – and never was. Except in one sense: she's mad as hell. She's been locked out of sight in a mental hospital for 60 years, with no justification or explanation. The injustice is beyond Esme's expression or Iris' comprehension. How

---

2 Maggie O'Farrell, *The Vanishing Act of Esme Lennox* (London: Tinder, 2006).

anyone could do this to another person cannot be imagined. It has to be seen to be believed.

To begin with the commitment to see does, of course, make one significant assumption: that when it comes to injustice, the person called to act justly does not principally identify themselves as the victim of injustice, or the perpetrator. The key word is 'principally'. We can take for granted that most if not all people are subject to some level of injustice, and many to a considerable level – the issue is, they are still approaching justice from the point of view of what they seek primarily for others. For a person who has lately emerged from a 25-year wrongful imprisonment, that is not the case. It is almost inevitable – and not wrong – that their first thought is of the injustice done to them. We can also take for granted that most if not all people are colluding in some degree of injustice inflicted on others – whether or not they are aware of it or would acknowledge it. The issue, again, is that they are approaching injustice from the point of view of one who is not principally defined by what they have been or are perpetrating against others. For a person who owns 2,000 houses and rents them at inflated rates to tenants who are not in a position to demand reasonable service for their payment, this is not the case. Such a person would best take the log out of their own eye before seeking to remove the splinter from another's.

That said, seeking justice for another may be a way of better coming to understand what justice might mean for oneself; and it may also mean coming to reflect humbly and transformatively on the injustice one has been or still is perpetrating. Which is why seeing justice, while it may seem to assume a safe vantage point of privilege, is not only that – but despite that, is still a good place to begin.

3

Recognize

Be careful when you call for justice; because one day, justice may call for you.

Perceiving justice has to involve, at or near the outset, recognizing one's own complicity in the habits and structures of injustice. Stieg Larsson, the author of the *Dragon Tattoo* novels that inspired the films about Lisbeth Salander, was haunted by an event from his youth. Aged 15, he witnessed a collective sexual assault made by three of his friends on a young girl. For the rest of his short life, which ended at 54, Larsson was plagued by self-hatred for failing to intervene to help the girl. For him, writing the novels required him to go back to the worst day of his life. His inaction that day left a scar on his character for which he never forgave himself. The novels are a fictionalized account of a Sweden neither he nor the Swedish public wanted to see or face up to – a land of far-right extremists, white supremacists and violent sexual predators. But writing the novels was never simply an act of accusation: it was always a recognition and confession that he himself was implicated in the underside of that culture.

Recognizing complicity means apprehending how deeply involved almost everyone is in either the processes or the benefits of injustice, and how difficult it is to extricate oneself from such culpability. Let's say you prepare to go on a march. You put on a T-shirt that proclaims words of protest. You take up a banner that calls for change. You text colleagues to arrange where to convene. You step into a car to set out on the day. But you may or may not know that your T-shirt was made by a child who, in order to sustain her family, has scarcely ever gone to school and may never have the chance to develop skills and fulfil potential; that the paper for your banner was made from trees in a non-sustainable forest, whose importation to your country required countless gallons of carbon-emitting non-renewable fuel; that the pens you used to write your banner were bought on special offer because the firm that produced them had been subject to a hostile takeover in which a legal loophole meant that all the original firm's employees lost their jobs and were not compensated for accumulated leave; that the materials used to make your smartphone were extracted from mines in a country where all the mineral companies are owned by foreign corporations that pay little or no tax and shore up an oppressive regime in order to maintain their fiscal and mercantile advantages; or that the hybrid car you're stepping into to join with others in protesting injustice consumed 40,000 gallons of water in its production alone. To resist one aspect of injustice, you're actively if not knowingly participating in several others.

The point is not simply to be renewed in developing a lifestyle that leaves the minimum ecological footprint and colludes in the least possible oppression in your own country or the world. The point is to cultivate the humility that accepts that it's almost impossible ever to be completely in the right – entirely on the side of justice, unimpeachable in one's noble intention and execution. Paul told the Romans that all have sinned and fallen

short of the glory of God. 'All' means all: it includes
those who strive earnestly to be free of such failings.
To act justly is not to entertain the fallacy that you can
make yourself righteous, or to imagine you can build
a perfect society through your own efforts. It's to find
hope in collaborating with others in becoming a better
person and seeking a better future, flawed as both will
inevitably be. The mistake is to remain under the illusion
that you can ever get it right. The same mistake underlies paralysis. Refusing ever to begin – in the knowledge
that you will inevitably make mistakes – is a form of
deferral that underwrites the same false notion that it is
possible to get it right, and you should wait until all your
attitudes and gestures are perfectly formed before beginning. Paralysis and self-righteousness have the same root
error – the error of the third slave in the parable of the
talents, who buried his gift in the ground rather than
risk taking it to market.[1]

This is especially pertinent when Christians call for
justice. For we live in an era when the injustices perpetrated by public representatives of the church, or by
others who used the protection of the church, and in
both cases too often actively hidden and repeatedly
denied – and thus condoned and exacerbated – by
the church, are being widely exposed and rightly condemned. Christians cannot shrug their shoulders and
say, 'It wasn't me.' All Christians share responsibility for
using their influence and example to change a culture,
learn to do better, bring perpetrators to face justice and
humbly seek to listen to and serve the interests of those
the church and its representatives have so badly failed.

---

1 Matthew 25.14–30.

Only if they do so will Christians ever earn the right to speak of justice again.

One of the most difficult forms of recognition is the willingness to change a story we have created when the facts turn out not to fit that story. The 2012 Danish film *The Hunt* is set in an idyllic Scandinavian town, perhaps not unlike Faha, the Irish village we encountered earlier. Lucas' life is fragile: his relationship with his ex-wife is poor, his access to his teenage son limited; but he has a tight group of male friends with whom he's grown up, and he has a steady job as a teacher at the local kindergarten. Suddenly everything changes when the director of the kindergarten speaks with Klara, a winsome member of Lucas' class, and the daughter of his best friend. The director, alert to a possible safeguarding concern, infers that Lucas has behaved inappropriately with Klara. Certain that children never lie about such things, the director informs all the parents of children in Lucas' class. In no time, Lucas is a pariah in the community, ostracized, assaulted and humiliated; his house is attacked, his dog killed. Finally, Lucas is arrested.

The story gathers bewildering momentum. The community jumps to the worst conclusion and cannot tolerate any contrasting information. Klara in fact never alleges sexual activity: she simply nods when adults verbalize possible culpable scenarios to her. Quickly she begins to say to her parents, 'I said something foolish' – but her mother assumes this is because she can't bear to dwell on the memory. Lucas' son never doubts his father and is furious with Klara and her family – and bears the cost of physical violence as a result. Eventually it comes to light that all the children in Lucas' class have alleged almost identical incidents taking place on the same sofa in his basement – yet his house doesn't have a basement. Lucas is consequently released from detention. Numerous other incidents cluster in: we recall Klara's brother showing her an indecent image on his iPad, which no doubt planted the idea; we remember Klara kissing Lucas on the lips, unsolicited, as a possible sign of her already-confused understanding of sexual contact; we recollect Klara's father saying to Lucas that he knew him so well he could always tell if he was lying; we appreciate the emotional impoverishment of the community, hidden within frequent bouts of male drunkenness and ostentatious display.

Yet even when Lucas' innocence is established, there's no sign that the community is willing to take responsibility for aspects of its culture that offered a fertile soil for false accusation. The film ends with Lucas walking in the woods, whereupon a rifle shot just misses his head. He can't tell who fired the shot. But the shot's message is clear: Lucas' reacceptance into the community is not complete and never will be. The community can't ever fully drop the version of the story it so rapidly adopted. Lucas will never cease to be a hunted man. The narrative is thus one of multiple levels of recognition: that a terrible thing can happen in a close community; that adults can ask a child leading questions, and take away a story they dread, but of which they are nonetheless hyper-aware; that a community can ignore all counter-evidence when carried along by a story; that justice, in the form of the declaration of innocence, can be done when that counter-evidence is heard and duly treated; but that justice, in the form of true restoration, genuine apology and the complete rebuilding of trust and relationship, may never be done.

Perhaps the most common form recognition takes today is found in the command, 'Check your privilege.'

Just as most campaigners for climate justice have to reckon with their own complicity in the climate crisis, so many who shout against discrimination today have to address the advantages they habitually take for granted, which constitute the soil in which discrimination prospers. For example, a Black person in Britain today may find a rented accommodation is no longer available once their identity comes to light; may be stopped by the police for no justifiable reason; may be asked to explain where they're 'really from'; may be asked to speak for all ethnic or racial minorities because they appear to be the only 'other' in the room; may find that if a family member loses their life or is seriously assaulted, the media pay very little attention to the story. A white British person may not see themselves as particularly advantaged socially or economically; but they are very unlikely to experience such endemic persecutions, not least because they have the privilege of invisibility. Privilege may not entail having significant wealth – being able to pay others to do menial domestic tasks, attending an elite school, taking exotic holidays or having access to private health care – it may simply mean not being subject to regular humiliation and not being made constantly aware of the scorn in which one's identity is widely held. Thus, pursuing justice may begin with coming to understand the privileged condition of having the freedom to seek justice while not being already immersed in a world of microaggressions and undermining social norms – a deal for which no person in healthy circumstances would settle.

But race and ethnicity are not the only pretext for unjust social norms. Demeaning everyday exchanges and systemic forms of exclusion remain common for many people on the grounds of gender, sex and sexuality; physical, cognitive, sensory or intellectual disability; age, appearance, height and figure; socio-economic class; and sometimes religion, such as the experience of Muslims after so-called Islamist terrorist attacks, of a Roman Catholic in a twentieth-century Belfast shipyard, or of an atheist in the nineteenth-century Westminster parliament. The configuration of identity across several of these signifiers is commonly known as intersectionality. Rather than fuelling an Oppression Olympics to establish reasons why one qualifies as the most persecuted, a matrix such as this instils awareness of how different aspects of identity can multiply experiences of exclusion. A person who examined this list deeply and found no area in which they tallied on the marginalized side of the equation might have good reason to pause before going out to pursue justice and consider whether justice might best be sought by aligning their efforts alongside colleagues or neighbours who experience life differently.

What all the examples I have cited have in common – the guilt of Stieg Larsson, the complicity of the protestor, the subtlety of privilege and the complexity of intersectionality – is the thread of irony. Irony is the factor instantly apparent to an attentive observer that can be totally lost on the passionate actor. An archetypal portrayal of the person so wholly committed to their pursuit of righteousness that they lose all sense of true justice is found in a novel that dwells on the urgency and pitfalls of justice: *Bleak House*. In chapter 4, Charles Dickens introduces us to Mrs Jellyby, who is devoted to placing 200 'healthy families cultivating coffee and educating the natives of Borrioboola-Gha on the left bank of the Niger', and spends her whole time 'in correspondence with public bodies, and with private individuals anxious for the welfare of their species all over the country'. The novel vividly describes how, in her passion for her cause, Mrs Jellyby fails to recognize that she has enslaved her daughter Caddy as her secretary, driven her husband to utter despair, expressed by banging his head against a stone wall, and subjected her younger children to emotional and physical neglect. Dickens is not reproducing traditional expectations of gender roles within the household; he is drawing an analogy with the England of his time, which was launching numerous imperialist escapades, justified by colonial benevolence and philanthropy, while allowing grotesque poverty to multiply at home. But anyone who perceives Mrs Jellyby as simply a figure of scorn and ridicule has missed Dickens' ulterior purpose: in her he proffers a mirror to anyone who supposes they can pursue justice, a mirror in which they may or may not see themselves, but should at least see those behind them whom, in their haste for righteousness, they have too readily and self-servingly neglected. Dickens would approve of the sentiment to be careful when you call for justice – lest justice call for you.

PART 2

Constructing Justice

The book is structured around a distinction between constructive justice, which seeks to create and inhabit a system that reliably achieves just outcomes, and corrective justice, sometimes known as social justice, which upholds the causes and people poorly served by constructive justice. This part of the book addresses the first of these. It looks at what it means to build a justice system through affirming conventions, each of which arises through a story. It emphasizes that underpinning any such system is an ethic, usually known as the rule of law, by which all in society submit to certain commitments and adhere to certain principles, without which justice quickly breaks down. And it focuses on the way these two dimensions depend on close scrutiny, lest the good that justice represents be subverted by the mistaken, the unobservant, the malign or the unfortunate. These three areas make up the three chapters that follow.

4

Build

In a 1960s stand-up routine, the comedian said, 'Years ago, my mother gave me a bullet. I put it in my breast pocket. Two years later, I was walking down Seventh Avenue, when a berserk evangelist hurled a Gideon Bible out of a hotel room window, hitting me in the chest. The Bible would have gone through my heart if it wasn't for that bullet.' I remembered that story some years ago when I interviewed a distinguished US judge. She talked about a night when she was mugged. As she recalled the incident, she said, 'My assailant couldn't find a wallet on me, but he did steal my most precious possession: a gold-embossed copy of the United States Constitution, which I kept in my breast pocket.' My mind was already back on the stand-up routine. But the judge went on, 'And d'you know what, when I told my colleague on the circuit what had happened, he reached into his pocket and got out an almost identical gold-embossed Constitution, and said, "Have it, from me."'

The most striking thing to me was the confidence the judge conveyed. She sincerely believed that the US Constitution contained the answer to every question a judge might have to face. If you couldn't find the answer, you simply hadn't tried hard enough. That constitutes a particular conception of justice. It perceives justice as a body of laws and precedents that, together with traditions, punishments and professional standards, constitute a legal system. That judge believed that her system, shaped by the US Constitution, had the answer to everything that really mattered.

Such a justice system cannot be created overnight. It requires the separation of powers between the legislative, executive and judiciary. It involves the establishment of institutions – not just law courts, but training, professional standards and remuneration for lawyers, judges, clerks and officers; a distinction between the police and the military, and a tradition of policing by consent; an honourable system of punishment, prisons, probation officers and a process of reintegrating ex-offenders into society. The mistake is to assume that such a system is identical with justice. But try establishing and maintaining justice without it. As the fourth-century theologian Augustine puts it, 'Justice being taken away, what are kingdoms but great robberies? For what are robberies themselves, but little kingdoms?'[1]

A legal system is an interconnected matrix of codes, such as laws, expectations and principles, together with collective cultures, such as institutions and professions, backed up by a process of education and training, protected and delivered by a system of enforcement, notably the police, the prison network, probation, witness protection and rehabilitation schemes, and the courts. None of these can function effectively without a wider culture of trust in the process and those who carry it out, and a general respect for the law. Yet none of these elements can prevent injustice occurring. What they can do is assure those who are its victims that every effort will be made to find culprits, bring them to face judgement

---

1 Augustine, *The City of God*, 4:4.

and due punishment, thus enacting a public statement of what constitutes right and wrong, thereby deterring those planning to perpetrate injustice.

The notion of seeking justice is, in practice, less often understood as following a legal process through from its outset to its conclusion. Instead, it is more widely perceived as addressing injustices that are overlooked, mishandled or perpetrated by those who enforce the law, fall outside the law as it currently exists (because they happen to take place in another country, or because they involve a scenario the law has not yet expanded to address), or have arisen within the processes of the law themselves. This imbalance of perception is something of an anomaly. Upholding a broadly functioning and generally respected justice system is a vital – perhaps *the* vital – component of justice in countries that maintain a general respect for the rule of law, and perhaps the most helpful institution to introduce to those that don't.

Such institutions don't fall fully formed from the sky. They never have, even in cultures that have come to take them for granted. For example, take a plaque tucked away on a wall near an old entrance to the most famous court in Britain, the Central Criminal Court of England and Wales, known as the Old Bailey after the street on which it stands.[2] The plaque commemorates a significant event that took place in 1670. William Penn was a busy man before he crossed the Atlantic and gave his name to Pennsylvania: he was a leader of the Quakers. At the time they were regarded as an illegal sect, unwilling to cooperate with the established church. Hence, they couldn't meet in any house of worship; so Penn led a

---

2 I am grateful to Michael Mainelli for telling me this story and giving me the opportunity to see the plaque in situ.

worship service for a handful of people on a quiet street. He and a colleague, William Mead, were arrested for taking part in an unlawful and tumultuous assembly. At their trial, Penn demanded to know on what law he was being indicted. 'For where there is no law, there is no transgression; and that law which is not in being, is so far from being common, that it is no law at all.' When the judge demurred, saying it took 30 or 40 years to study the common law, Penn added, 'If the common law be so hard to understand, it is far from being common.'

The judge was furious with Penn and instructed the jury to find the defendants guilty. The jury pronounced them not guilty. Not content, the judge sent them away to consider a different verdict. When they returned the same verdict, the judge demanded from Bushnell, the jury's spokesperson, 'a verdict that the court will accept, and you shall be locked up without meat, drink, fire, and tobacco. We will have a verdict by the help of God or you will starve for it.' The rigmarole was repeated three further times, after which the jury refused to go out for a sixth time. The judge fined them and imprisoned Penn and Mead for contempt of court. Eventually a writ of habeas corpus gained release for all involved. The jurors sued the mayor and judge, and won. It was concluded that judges 'may try to open the eyes of the jurors, but not lead them by the nose'. Sometimes known as the Bushnell trial, the case became a landmark moment in the history of British justice. Thereafter juries would have the right to give their verdict according to their convictions.

Four centuries later, four people were put on trial for toppling a statue of the benefactor Edward Colston, also a notorious slave trader, and plunging it into the River Avon at the Bristol docks on 7 June 2020, amid a crowd of 3,000 people. They were charged with destroying or harming property under the Criminal Damage Act 1971. The defendants maintained they had a 'lawful excuse', arguing that they acted reasonably (not least because the statue was dragged across the cobbles where so many had been hauled against their will centuries before). The Colston Four were acquitted by the 12 jurors: thus affirming that the power of the state to punish and imprison is only to be used when the circumstances are clear.[3]

On top of the dome above the Old Bailey stands a bronze statue of Lady Justice, scales in her right hand and a sword in her left. Personifying justice in this way enhances the notion that it is an absolute – that justice can definitively be arrived at and, once achieved, all other virtues and blessings will follow. Movements for social justice, while they've largely moved on from bronze statues, tend to the same view: justice is an abstract goal that, once attained, yields all other goods. The Bushnell trial suggests that justice is not an abstract goal – it is instead a set of conventions, arrived at through earnest striving for good order and universal well-being. Pure justice is an idol; there's very little that's pure about human relations gone so badly wrong as to involve the courts. Establishing good conventions is the heart of justice, and those conventions, far from being luminous and eternal, are always in need of updating and refining. Justice is a system, not an ideal; a best attempt, not

---

3 For an incisive treatment, see Graeme Hayes, Brian Doherty and Steven Cammiss, 'We attended the trial of the Colston four: here's why their acquittal should be celebrated', *The Conversation*, 7 January 2022, https://theconversation.com/we-attended-the-trial-of-the-colston-four-heres-why-their-acquittal-should-be-celebrated-174481, accessed 14.1.2022.

perfection. Conventions aren't abstract; they each presume a story. The stories in this chapter and throughout this book illustrate that claim.

That best attempt is refined by a series of challenges. The strengths and weaknesses of such a process of refinement are illustrated by the case of James Somerset. He was an enslaved African who was purchased by Charles Stewart, a customs officer, in Boston, Massachusetts, and brought to England in 1769. Two years later Somerset escaped. Following his recapture a month later, Stewart imprisoned him in a ship bound for Jamaica. Somerset's godparents applied for a writ of habeas corpus, claiming that he was being held unlawfully. It was maintained that unlike its colonies, England had no law that recognized slavery; that no person could enslave himself, and no contract could bind a man without his consent. While lawyers for Stewart advised caution lest the principle of property be abrogated and lest the 15,000 enslaved people then in Britain also be freed, Somerset's cause prevailed.

The strengths of the legal process, as disclosed by this case, are that Somerset walked free and that the principle that no one be held unlawfully against their will, a tenet tracing back to Henry II's Assize of Clarendon in the twelfth century, was upheld. The rather pompous claim from one of Somerset's lawyers, that 'this air is too pure for a slave to breathe in', became associated with the case. The weaknesses were that the ruling neither made nor was asked to make any sweeping judgement against slavery. Somerset was freed on a series of carefully coded legal technicalities, so construed as to have no bearing on the widespread ownership of slaves across several British colonies (at that time still including America). The judge did not even say that a slave became free by entering England. And yet the arguments rehearsed in this case became crucial in the later abolition of the slave trade, and of slavery in the British Empire, and influential in the debate in the USA still later. Thus, this was no case of justice in any abstract sense – that no one may have any right to call another person their property – but in terms of the growth of convention, and the emergence of consensus against the condition of slavery, and the freedom of this one man, it was a step towards justice.[4]

Building a justice system involves the meticulous process of establishing conventions, modifying according to precedent and establishing roles, such that if each key party plays their role appropriately, precedent is carefully followed and conventions are upheld, justice should be done. This is not a portrayal of justice as campaigning or exposing; it's one in which there's an honoured place for the clerk to the court, the police officer, prison officer, probation officer, barrister, solicitor and judge: to carry out each of these roles with thoroughness, honour and dignity is to serve justice and ensure justice is done. Each of these roles continues to evolve, just as the Bushnell trial and the Somerset case set vital precedents for subsequent justice to follow.

One important convention is the recognition that the victim of a crime is not the best judge of the most appropriate punishment. A poignant insight from those campaigning on behalf of prisoners on death row in the United States is that bereaved families are made to feel that if they do not pursue the death penalty for the killer of their loved one (whatever the perpetrator's

---

4 For further reflections on the significance of this point, see David Olusoga, *Black and British: A Forgotten History* (London: Pan, 2016), pp. 127–41.

circumstances, however unsafe or in some cases racially biased the conviction might be), then it indicates they did not truly love their child. Such a distortion of what love entails demonstrates the importance of punishment lying with an authority entirely separate from the influence of the aggrieved party, however serious the offence and however profound their hurt or grief may be. The conviction of the offender is often a significant part of the victim's or victim's bereaved family's journey towards acceptance and some degree of peace; but it is in no sense the whole of that journey. Vengeance is what a justice system exists to prevent, not to embody.

Thus, an ordered system of justice depends on establishing and adhering to conventions. But what if those conventions evolve in ways that don't serve justice? Sometimes conventions become accepted even though they perpetuate violence or vengeance. The problem with looking into the London sky to see the bronze Lady Justice is not just that pursuing abstract ideals wastes energy that could be spent developing good examples or better conventions: it's that justice looks down to the ground at least as much as up to the sky. In the basement of the Old Bailey lie the tiny, windowless cells in which prisoners awaiting trial are kept. Depriving people of their liberty, and in many cases keeping them in torturously confined spaces for long periods, isn't pure justice: it's a convention – and a convention that shames our societies. Deportation detention centres can be even worse. Much attention is given, rightly, to the disproportionate balance of who comes to be incarcerated, and to the way the prison population reflects the inequalities of our societies more generally. But too little attention is directed to the nature and purpose of incarceration itself.

In its early days, the Old Bailey dispensed summary justice. Punishments such as whipping, branding and the pillory or stocks dealt with crimes instantly. Today we decry such things as inhuman and degrading. But why do we not feel the same about locking a person up for years on end? How do we tolerate the extended periods for which the accused can be kept in such conditions, whether through internment or on remand, before a conviction that may never come? And what are we to do with those who, while their crimes are heinous, are little more than children when those crimes are committed, and face half a lifetime as adults imprisoned for a crime committed when they were too young to face adult levels of accountability?

Some conventions are well overdue a wholesale review. Incarceration for public protection still has a role. But its use as retribution or deterrent is outdated, expensive, counterproductive and a source of shame – less for the prisoner than for society as a whole. It begs the question of whether prison today is a dimension of the justice system or an institutionalization of injustice. The name 'penitentiary' discloses that prisons were originally part of a process of transformation, regeneration and re-habilitation. It's hard to see how today's prisons advance those goals. But somehow incarceration falls outside conventional campaigns for justice. When justice is perceived as the rectification of wrong, it adopts a limited narrative that begins when that wrong was perpetrated. The narrative seldom embraces the circumstances that foster the resentment and rage that provide the most fertile soil for wrongdoing. Nothing fosters resentment and rage more surely than incarceration. Thus the flaws of incarceration are not just an indication that justice understood as evolving convention is inadequate; they are a sign that a story that begins with the perpetration of a crime is beginning in the wrong place.

And this exposes the convention that lies within the process of justice. Justice is the procedure by which an offender is held to account, and, if found beyond reasonable doubt to be in the wrong, faces redress, while the victim, if there is one, is vindicated and the law reasserted. This process operates by isolating an incident, examining it in detail and excluding all other information that might be interesting but is not strictly relevant. The flaw in such a convention is that it suggests you can only establish justice if you limit your understanding of truth. It may be just that a woman is punished for killing her domestic partner, because the law asserts that killing is wrong; but if the domestic partner's long campaign of control, humiliation and subjugation is ruled out of consideration, the narrowing of the case to the single violent incident constitutes the assertion of one kind of justice at the expense of another.

It's at this point that we need to distinguish between legal justice and social justice. There should be no difference: legal justice should also be social justice; justice is a social virtue. But as we have seen, justice is a set of conventions that presume a story and it tends to proceed by focusing on just one part of that story. Social justice identifies what is lost by focusing on that one part. Social justice refers to the process of recognizing the extent to which widespread and endemic inequality inhibits the well-being of many, campaigning for social transformation to eradicate it, and the creation of conditions for all to flourish without fear of oppression. Thus, social justice demands that the rest of the story, excluded in order to enable legal justice to isolate a matter that can be decided, be ushered back in. Social justice tends to be more inclined towards identifying and campaigning against varieties of injustice: consequently, it never rests, since it constantly sees more injustice out there to address. By contrast, legal justice seeks the happy place where justice has been done and has been seen to be done.

For these reasons it may seem that justice and social justice, far from being complementary (or even identical), are in significant respects contradictory or mutually exclusive. Yet try seeking social justice when you have no reliable system of justice to fall back on. Hence one of the key challenges of seeking justice is to establish a way of pursuing both justice and social justice at the same time, without undermining either.

5

Practise

You can have all the laws and rulings in the world, yet still be a long way from justice. That's because without the rule of law, good judgements are useless. Practising justice means that everyone, including monarchs, lawmakers, judges and the military, is subject to the law. But it also requires that you have a disciplined and trustworthy police force, able to apply the law, and a culture of respect for the law among the general public. It's a huge problem if the rate of conviction for sexual assaults hovers around two per cent. There's no point having elaborate laws about breaking and entering if everyone knows the police won't investigate minor burglaries. It's no use having careful protections for the right to assembly or freedom of speech if there's a tyrant in power who can arrest and imprison and disappear people at will. It's no good having a high and mighty legal system if its language, procedures and costs make it inaccessible to ordinary people. A stop-and-search law that's disproportionately used against one section of the population does more harm than good. In relation to the civil law, it's vital that a contract can be enforced and that those who breach agreements or other such duties recompense those who suffer loss. A society cannot impose strict regulations around social distancing or numbers gathering during a pandemic if it turns out senior politicians and civil servants act as though the rules don't apply to them. You've nowhere to turn when the police are as corrupt as the gangsters. Thus, the rule of law extends to every station of life.

The physical embodiment of the rule of law is the police force. Home Secretary Robert Peel established the Metropolitan Police in 1829 in recognition that London was a city of unprecedented size in global history. His initiative included several key decisions. The officers would be paid; they would be visibly distinct from the military (blue uniforms, not red); they would be politically neutral, not agents of the ruling government; their effectiveness would be measured by their ability to deter crime, not arrest criminals; they would operate by consent of the public; the public would bestow authority on them and would hold them accountable. Appropriate training, conditions and remuneration have always been as vital as accountability in fostering a body of people held high in public trust and esteem; appropriately, the role of overseeing the police is more about ensuring there is no incentive to do wrong than catching and punishing those who nonetheless stray.

All of which means that a complete failure in the culture of a police force constitutes a catastrophic event for justice and for society as a whole. The Sarah Everard case in London in March 2021 illustrates the disastrous damage done when the rule of law is abrogated in this particular way. When her murderer was tried, and pleaded guilty, it came to light that he was a police officer who'd used his power of arrest during lockdown to handcuff her on the pretext that she was breaking the pandemic curfew. But this allegation was simply a cover for his being able to perpetrate his terrible crimes against her. The case not only highlighted the vulnerability of

women on London streets at night but, more explicitly, it undermined public trust in the police as a whole,
since it turned out that one officer had used the authority given to him to execute his criminal purpose. How
many other officers like him were lurking in the ranks
of the police, waiting to take advantage of members of
the public with sinister intent? Thus does the rule of
law fracture, not just through its casual bypassing by
many, but through its terrible flouting by one trusted
to enforce it. The fact that those gathering for a vigil
in Sarah's memory (and to express their own fear and
dismay) were dispersed due to the threat of spreading
the Covid-19 virus only compounded the damage done
to the rule of law in this case, for the police collectively
were seen to be swallowing a camel and straining at a
gnat – and thus to have their priorities and perception of
risk completely in the wrong place. That the same police
force subsequently proved reluctant to investigate evident breaches of Covid regulations at 10 Downing Street
invited comparisons that further eroded trust.

Such an egregious failure explains why many people
put their faith in and commit their life to ensuring good
order. Good order means a society that doesn't just
have good laws but also has trustworthy law enforcement, freedom of the press, independent institutions and
a strong ethic of public service. Together such robust
guarantees create a law-abiding culture. Freedom of the
press is itself of little use unless the press holds itself to a
standard of seeking truth, rather than spreading gossip,
propagating slander or undermining public trust. This
is why debates and test cases about the public interest
are so significant. The rule of law can be upheld when
a journalist uses somewhat devious and even underhand tactics to gain information that a senior figure

has seriously misled the legislature or the public as a whole; but the rule of law is impoverished when such an approach is used to shame or humiliate a person on matters that have no bearing on the genuine well-being of society. There's a significant difference between what the public is interested in and what is in the public interest. The same principle applies to the prosecution of cases that might have political or vindictive purposes but advance no genuine public benefit: good order demands that no such cases be permitted.

Good order is not simply about impeccable and accountable public institutions. More broadly, ensuring good order rests with civil society. What voluntary organizations and associations, faith groups, single-interest pressure groups, charities, schools, universities, hospitals, the media and similar institutions have in common is that they're not part of the justice or governmental system, but neither are they primarily driven by commercial imperatives. Perhaps more than any other part of society, such organizations develop the kind of culture that ensures the rule of law is taken for granted and failures of the justice system are challenged. Professional or volunteer members of such groups may then act justly, not simply by using their position to advocate for a particular issue, case or cause, but by fostering a culture that has a healthy understanding of what constitutes normal.

We may briefly note two ways of doing this. The first is, when the surrounding 'normal' is unjust, to offer a better alternative within civil society. More constructive than protest (though not always possible) is to offer a working example of what would be better. With the outbreak of the First World War, the Suffragist movement had to find new, less confrontational, outlets to advance the cause of women's suffrage.[1] In 1914, Flora Murray and Louisa Garrett Anderson approached the French Embassy with the idea of creating a field hospital in Wimereux, near Calais. (Anderson had served four weeks in Holloway prison for her participation in suffrage protests.) They recruited enough medically trained women to staff it. In 1915, that hospital was transferred to Endell Street in Covent Garden, London. The Endell hospital had 573 beds. Over the five years it was active, 26,000 patients were cared for and 20 operations per day was common. Women worked not only as nurses and clerks, but as drivers, dentists, pathologists and surgeons. Women doctors received the pay and benefits of military ranks from lieutenant to lieutenant colonel; but they themselves had no rank and they were not permitted to command men. Endell doctors published seven articles in the medical journal *The Lancet*. These were the first hospital-based research papers by British female doctors.

The hospital was closed in October 1919. Medical schools once again closed their doors to female students. Female doctors were shunted into low-paid, low-status jobs. Winston Churchill, the Secretary of State for War, refused to give female army doctors equal military rank. The Endell episode in the story of women's emancipation closed; but the fact that women could perform the role of senior physician at least as well as men had been proved beyond contradiction.

The other approach is to reinforce healthy cultural norms by highlighting occasions when they've been

---

[1] Wendy Moore, *Endell Street: The Women Who Ran Britain's Trailblazing Military Hospital* (London: Atlantic, 2020). I am grateful to Gail Davey for bringing this story to my attention.

contravened, ensuring that they're not ignored, where ignoring norms may seem to be a form of tolerance, but in fact slowly erodes the rule of law. In the Revd W. Awdry story *Henry the Green Engine*, one character says to another of the indulgence of whistling while going through tunnels, 'There's nothing wrong; but we just don't do it.' During their infamous cricket tour of Australia in 1930–31, the England fast bowlers employed the 'bodyline' tactic of bowling fearsome deliveries that the Australian batsmen couldn't avoid, and placed fielders to catch their involuntary prods. This was not technically illegal; but everyone perceived it to be against the spirit of the game. Hence the expression, 'It's just not cricket.'

Indeed, one indicator of the vibrancy of good order in contemporary society is the attention given to sharp practice in visible sports controversies. We may consider three examples. When close viewing of television footage of the Australian cricket team in Cape Town in 2018 highlighted that one of the players was using sandpaper to rough up one side of the ball, it triggered a national scandal. Few believed it to be an isolated incident. Attention focused on the captain and vice-captain, and the way they had instructed a junior member of the team to perpetrate the offence. What ensued, besides lengthy bans, was widespread introspection about the nature of leadership in a win-at-all-costs culture. While it seemed hypocritical for past cricketers to rise in condemnation, as if such practice was new, the evidence was incontrovertible and the punishment inevitable.

By contrast, in the Argentina vs England quarter-final at the World Cup in 1986, when Diego Maradona rose above the advancing England goalkeeper to punch the ball into the net, the incident was not spotted by the referee and no punishment was exacted afterwards. It was manifestly unjust; the whole world could see it; but the convention that the referee's decision is final overrode the visible transgression of the rule. Lexi Thompson's experience was different. Three shots clear with six holes to play in the final round of the first major tournament of 2017 in Rancho Mirage, California, she was deducted four shots when a television viewer pointed out she'd incorrectly replaced her ball before a one-foot putt the previous day. She finished second. In this case, the absurd severity of the penalty for what seemed a minor and unintentional aberration brought scorn upon the rules. But though it seemed terribly unfair, it was not unjust: no one suggested the rules should be ignored.

The lively debate such incidents evoke indicates the depth to which the rule of law pervades a culture. When you reach the point that people shrug their shoulders at the flouting of a universally understood rule or convention, you know the rule of law is in serious trouble. This is how civil society provides public tests of the health of a culture. In a similar way, the integrity of schools in providing fair and accurate grades for their pupils to the public educational authorities during the Covid-19 pandemic was a litmus test of the probity of the whole system on which public education depends.

It's important to recognize the vital role of trade unions as key constituents of civil society. The flourishing of trade unions ensures that no one can ever assume justice can be dictated from the perspective of the owner, the controller, the wealthy. It also confirms that justice will always have a collective element and never devolve into the contested claims of competing individuals. Unions enable their members to attain the power as a collective they could never aspire to alone. Union representatives uphold justice in a number of ways, usually seeking to establish the good rather than mitigating or prosecuting the bad. These can include ensuring fair working conditions, rewards and opportunities for training or education, supporting members in the face of sickness, disciplinary measures or redundancy, and assisting with legal or financial difficulties. Unions have significantly enhanced the well-being of workers through achieving minimum-wage legislation, eradicating child labour, improving parental leave and promoting equality.

Advocacy for the rule of law has not always been consistent. Notoriously in the era of slavery and segregation in the United States, the emphasis on good order came at the expense of equality under the law for Americans, rather than as a determination to introduce it. The Civil Rights movement of the 1950s and 60s was a campaign to assert such equality; but the Black Lives Matter movement was a furious statement that, as late as the 2020s, it still seemed neither a reality for African Americans nor even a pressing aspiration for many, perhaps even most, in their own country. The apartheid regime justified its retention of power in South Africa in the 1970s and 80s by arguing that it was the only force in the country with any capacity to uphold the rule of law; that argument turned out to be wrong. The story of Ireland until the late twentieth century was of a consistent inability to ensure both Catholics and Protestants were treated equally in employment, housing and the legal system – injustices that lay closer to the root of the Troubles than any desire for a united Ireland. Martin Luther King's words, 'Injustice anywhere is a threat to justice everywhere', are, in simple terms, a statement that the murder of an African American in Minnesota is a warning bell to African Americans in every state of the union; but in more general terms, it is a recognition that, once the rule of law is breached, everyone is the loser.

Returning to *Bleak House*, we see Charles Dickens describing the interminable case in the Court of Chancery known as Jarndyce vs Jarndyce, brought about because a testator had left conflicting wills, which eventually exhausts the value of the entire estate. The case becomes a whirlpool into which members of the family are sucked and from which they can never extricate themselves. It is thought to have been partly inspired by an actual case that began in 1797 and was not resolved until 1859 (after the novel was published).[2] The novel illustrates the phrase 'justice delayed is justice denied', quoted by William Ewart Gladstone in Parliament in 1868 and by Martin Luther King in his 'Letter from Birmingham Jail' in 1963. The phrase is first found in the *Pirkei Avot*, or Sayings of the Fathers, which is part of the Jewish Mishnah. The problem was especially pertinent during the Covid-19 pandemic, when numerous cases were postponed due to the difficulty of appearing in person in court – including family cases, where the passage of time could be especially distressing.

The issue of delay is put in a wider context of threats to the rule of law in these remarks by Chief Justice of the United States Warren E. Burger to the American Bar Association in 1970:

> A sense of confidence in the courts is essential to maintain the fabric of ordered liberty for a free people; and three things could destroy that confidence and do incalculable damage to society: that people come to believe that inefficiency and delay will drain even a

---

2 For an alternative Victorian treatment of the shortcomings of the law, see Anthony Trollope's 1862 novel *Orley Farm*.

just judgment of its value; that people who have long been exploited in the smaller transactions of daily life come to believe that courts cannot vindicate their legal rights from fraud and over-reaching; that people come to believe the law – in the larger sense – cannot fulfil its primary function to protect them and their families in their homes, at their work, and on the public streets.[3]

These words illustrate the wide ramifications of just one aspect of the breach of the rule of law.

Two key issues with law, as we've seen, are how to establish a good system and what to do when a system doesn't produce a good outcome. Tom Bingham addressed both these issues by defining the rule of law as follows: 'That all persons and authorities within the state, whether public or private, should be bound by and entitled to the benefit of laws publicly and prospectively promulgated and publicly administered in the courts.' He then offered eight criteria to support that aspiration. They were that (1) The law must be accessible, intelligible, clear and predictable. (2) Questions of legal right and liability should ordinarily be resolved by the exercise of the law and not the exercise of discretion. (3) Laws should apply equally to all. (4) Ministers and public officials must exercise the powers conferred in good faith, fairly, for the purposes for which they were conferred – reasonably and without exceeding the limits of such powers. (5) The law must afford adequate protection of fundamental human rights. (6) The state must provide a way of resolving disputes that the parties

---

3 The full text is available at Warren E. Burger, 'The state of the judiciary – 1970', *American Bar Association Journal* 56/10, October 1970, https://www.jstor.org/stable/25725265, accessed 31.12.2021.

cannot themselves resolve. (7) The adjudicative procedures provided by the state should be fair. (8) The rule
of law requires compliance by the state with its obli-
gations in international as well as national laws.[4]

A crucial point about this list is that it provides
security against a government that legitimately claims
to conform to the rule of law, yet nonetheless oppresses
minorities, fails to outlaw slavery and affirms sexual
inequality. This is where principle (5) above really
matters.[5] A state that follows its own laws, but whose
laws do not enshrine the protection of fundamental
human rights, cannot claim to be upholding the rule of
law. Examples would be the apartheid regime in South
Africa and the Russian state today. In such societies a
person may be deprived of liberty, livelihood and even
life, while a vestigial legislative and judicial process pro-
tects the appearance of legal respectability. The outcome
of a genuine rule of law is not just that the guilty are
convicted – but that the innocent are not.[6] Meanwhile,
civil justice must be fair, swift and accessible.

---

4 Tom Bingham, *The Rule of Law* (London: Allen Lane,
2010). For a similarly influential US treatment, see Lon Fuller,
The Morality of Law (New Haven, CT: Yale University Press,
1964).

5 Although rights still turn out to be a moveable feast: the
European Court of Human Rights, for example, still allows
a significant latitude to convention states in the equality of
LGBTQ+ people before the law, reflecting the disparity of social
attitudes between western and eastern Europe.

6 Dominic Grieve, 'The rule of law and the prosecutor',
Gov.uk, 9 September 2013, https://www.gov.uk/government/
speeches/the-rule-of-law-and-the-prosecutor, accessed 23.12.2021.
Speech given at the 18th Annual Conference and General Meeting of the International Association of Prosecutors, Moscow.
I am grateful to Frances Stratton for drawing my attention to
this telling speech.

But the rule of law requires not just the right laws: it needs prosecutors of character to administer those laws. This is where principle (7) comes into play. Impartiality and fairness can't simply be legislated – they have to be lived, and are rooted in an ethos that cherishes a flourishing society and subdues desire for personal gain. Fairness means the prosecutor not allowing the state to determine what is legal, but remaining independent and making an evaluation on what the law says and what the evidence suggests. That evidence must be appropriately gained (not through torture or devious means) and its preparation is a vital part of just process. There is no place for settling political scores or advancing political agendas; neither is there a place for seeking career advancement or personal reward. Fairness also requires that the prosecutor must declare to the defendant evidence that weakens the prosecution's case; that the prosecutor must keep an open mind; and that the defendant has sufficient time to prepare an adequate defence, and for that defence to be heard. It also means that both sides of the argument have equal opportunity to be aired, and that each have the chance to challenge the other's case. Just societies need to be made up of just people: fairness is the characteristic that enables a set of reasonable laws to become the basis of a just society.[7]

What is missing from Tom Bingham's list is a recognition that the vulnerable and impoverished may find access to the law very difficult. It is fundamental to

---

7 Reflecting soberly on the British experience of using internment (that is, imprisonment without trial) in Northern Ireland, Grieve comments, 'If you undermine or subvert the rule of law in the belief that by so doing you will protect your regime or system of government, you will ultimately prove to be the destroyer of all that you seek to preserve.'

the rule of law that everyone have equal access to the law, and that is not the case if the cost of taking legal action or of mounting a defence is beyond the capacity of an individual to pay. The defenceless in the Old Testament were the widow, the orphan and the stranger; today they are the asylum seeker, the person with mental health difficulties, those with learning difficulties, those without access to the internet and those whose English-language skills are not developed. If the rule of law is to be genuinely upheld, establishing how people in such circumstances gain proper representation and are equally heard and understood must not be afterthoughts, but central considerations. Stipulation (3), that laws should apply equally for all, needs to be expanded to add, 'and justice must be *available* equally for all'.

The rule of law is always liable to be invoked in circumstances of oppression, since it can so readily serve as an ideological cover for one group lording it over others. Thus, Wendell Berry eloquently describes how the rule of law comes to be suspended in the politest of societies. He describes the moral predicament of the early nineteenth-century master in the American South who sits in church with his slaves, 'thus attesting his belief in the immortality of the soul of people whose bodies he owned and used'. Such a person 'had to perfect an empty space in his mind, a silence, between heavenly concerns and earthly concerns'. Berry thus identifies how churches came to devote themselves 'exclusively and obsessively with the question of [eternal] salvation', and not 'how best to live on earth'. The way to heaven was not by obeying the moral imperatives of Scripture, but by believing. Thus, in this Southern pietism, 'the mystical aspects of Christianity completely overshadow the moral' – but it's a bogus mysticism, 'a recipe by which to secure the benefits of eternal bliss without having to give up the benefits of temporal vice'. Because such churches focused entirely on sins such as drinking, failure to attend church and so-called immorality, 'the great moral tasks of honesty and peace and neighbourliness and brotherhood and the care of the earth have been left to be taken up on the streets by the "alienated" youth of the 1960s and 1970s.'[8]

What Berry provides is a lacerating analysis of how a proudly and avowedly Christian society can be as adept in circumventing the rule of law as any other – and how it can distort Christianity in doing so. He laments how, in the time of slavery and segregation, and still today, 'the religious institutions became comfort stations for scribes and publicans and pharisees. Far from curing the wound of racism, the white man's Christianity has been its soothing bandage.'[9] Thus, investment in the earnest establishment and vigilant maintenance of the rule of law is by no means a distraction from or alternative to Christian discipleship, ministry and mission. Instead, it is integral to fostering a culture in which faithful Christianity may be upheld and practised – and its distortions exposed and eradicated.

---

8 Wendell Berry, *The Hidden Wound* (Berkeley, CA: Counterpoint, 1989), pp. 16–18. Originally published in 1970.

9 Berry, *The Hidden Wound*, pp. 18–19.

6

Scrutinize

The third element of constructing justice is scrutiny. The popular image of justice is of a lawyer standing beside her client outside a courthouse, surrounded by journalists and cameras, announcing the transformative significance for a whole class of oppressed people of a case won against all odds in the face of precedent, indifference and hostility; of a woman leaving prison after years of incarceration for a crime she didn't commit, or a man stepping out into fresh air when his lawyer has proved the state had no right to detain him without trial. But justice involves just as much the detailed work of checking process, ensuring a sentence is served, inspecting prisons, evaluating the syllabus of training institutions and certifying professionals as of good character and due competence. Not only are many legal cases won and lost on precise details, but the whole legal system relies on the same rigour being applied to procedure as to argumentation, to the correction of error as to the establishment of fact, to the keeping of records as to the persuading of juries.

That level of scrutiny is particularly pertinent when it comes to one of the most troubling questions of justice: relating to a far-away regime that's evidently perpetrating frequent atrocities on its own people. There's a consensus of what citizens in the West hope for from such troubled countries: democracy, respect for human rights and the rule of law are aspirations for all people everywhere. When leaders are committed to such values, those agitating can focus on where a government falls short of its own standards. But what do you do if a regime doesn't flinch when confronted with evidence that it has tortured and murdered its own civilians? How do you avoid a powerless wringing of hands from afar?

In a case like this – and there are so many – working for justice principally means documenting incidences of injustice. Most regimes of this kind collapse under international censure and economic sanctions, domestic protest and journalistic evidence. The role of the journalist is to tell the story of what's taking place and hold it beside the story of justice – and let the reader decide how close the one is to the other. By such means the likelihood is that one day the junta that controls a country with a weak history of democratic structures will be held to account. When that day comes, it is photographs, videos and paper records that will provide compelling evidence against them. If you trust in the power of scrutiny, even in the face of overwhelming odds, there isn't 'nothing you can do'. You can carefully compile testimony, keep detailed records and communicate with supporters. That way, as external and internal pressure grows, the perpetrators of terrible crimes can be brought to face the truth. Perhaps only if leaders fear such a day in the future will they limit their misuse of power in the present. Sometimes you best deter an oppressor by saying, 'I'm watching you.'

The Amnesty International 'Write for Rights' campaign is an example of this 'watching'. It began in Poland with a group of activists who wrote letters all day and through the night for a full 24 hours on behalf of oppressed people whose names they knew. It now involves five million letters, tweets and signatures on petitions, all of which say to those who are tortured, harassed or unjustly imprisoned, 'I see you' – and to their persecutors, 'I'm watching you.' Social media offers immense power on behalf of hitherto silent peoples who can find ways to upload information or videos that disclose their plight without revealing their identity or precise whereabouts. Scrutiny of this kind is far from the most eye-catching form of asserting justice, but it's one of the most effective.

Ida B. Wells was freed by the Emancipation Proclamation during the American Civil War. In the 1890s, she embarked on a rigorous and extensive programme of research into the widespread practice of lynching in the Southern United States. In 1892 she published *Southern Horrors: Lynch Law in All its Phases*. This publication had two profound effects. It exposed and discredited the ubiquitous allegation that African American men posed a sexual threat to white women (noting that the real threat was, and always had been, the opposite: the danger white men frequently posed to African American women); and it named the true fear that underlay the programme of lynching – namely, the rise of African American economic independence, which the use of poll taxes and literacy tests had failed to inhibit. Three years later Wells published a 100-page pamphlet, *The Red Record*, pointing out the countless lynchings that had taken place since the Civil War and explaining that, prior to the Civil War, lynching was not as widely practised because the death of every African American carried a financial penalty to the slaveholder. Deliberately using information gleaned from white publications, Wells offered 14 pages of statistics and provided graphic accounts of specific lynchings, noting that prosecutions of white perpetrators almost never took place. Wells embodied the scrutiny on which good order and the rule of law depend.[1]

Scrutiny is a form of accountability. When an egregious failure – a huge loss of life, a terrible accident, a long-running catalogue of exploitation – takes place or comes to light, pointing the finger at one or two individuals seems inadequate and superficial. This is a disaster on a much larger scale and an indication that a whole series of processes have been abrogated or found wanting. Despite the expense and the patience required, what needs to follow is a major independent inquiry. Such a procedure isn't part of the construction of law, or the pursuit of law, but the repair of the breach when it's become obvious that the law alone isn't enough. Justice requires vigilance: it needs people prepared to track back and find precisely what went wrong, and whether the problem was deliberate evasion, human error, legal loophole or regulatory inadequacy.

The 2019 film *Dark Waters* dramatizes the true story of corporate lawyer Rob Bilott, who in 1998 learns of the plight of Wilbur Tennant, a humble West Virginia farmer. Wilbur's land is being contaminated by the giant pharmaceutical firm DuPont. The local authorities, the local population (which depends on DuPont for employment) and the systems of law and government, not to mention corporate complicity, are all stacked against Wilbur; but on searching innumerable boxes of evidence, Rob establishes that the local chemical plant, in manufacturing a chemical required for the production

---

1 See Ida B. Wells, *Crusade for Justice: The Autobiography of Ida B. Wells* (2nd edn, Chicago, IL: University of Chicago Press, 2020).

of Teflon, is poisoning the drinking water of 70,000 people. This is leading to kidney and testicular cancer and many other diseases. It becomes clear that DuPont has been aware for many decades that the chemicals were dangerous – but has carried on regardless. Rob takes out a class-action suit, and in 2017 wins a $671 million settlement on behalf of more than 3,500 plaintiffs. Since 2017, Rob Bilott has continued his campaign against other organizations that have carried on producing related chemicals, despite knowing of their harmful effects.[2]

In the defining scene in the film, Rob demands evidence from DuPont, and the company, determined both ostensibly to comply yet also find a way to halt the investigation, sends truckloads of relevant documents. Rob sits on the floor of a large warehouse, completely surrounded by intimidating boxes, and begins his solitary quest to discover the truth. The scene embodies the necessity and the cost of scrutiny.

Likewise, any justice system must assume there will be miscarriages of justice. When there's a dangerous incident on a plane, the pilot makes a detailed note and ensures the information is widely shared. No scar of blame is attached: what matters is the collective learning. The same practice is part of the code of conduct of surgeons. The same needs to be true of the justice system. While it may seem very much in one party's interest for a case to come out in an unjust way, the common good requires that all miscarriages be revisited,

---

2 Alejandro de la Garza, '*Dark Waters* tells the true story of the lawyer who took DuPont to court and won. But Rob Bilott's fight is far from over', *Time*, 25 November 2019, https://time.com/5737451/dark-waters-true-story-rob-bilott/, accessed 26.12.2021.

addressed and, if necessary and possible, retried. Rather than an extraordinary exception, fought for against all odds, and the cause of shame or disgrace, it should be an accepted possibility in every case, regarded as integral to justice, not an isolated rectification of injustice.

One poignant case is that of Sally Clark, a solicitor living in Cheshire, whose two sons both died within weeks of their birth, in December 1996 and January 1998, respectively. In both cases Sally was at home alone with the baby, and there was evidence of trauma – perhaps attributable to attempts at resuscitation. Initially both parents were arrested on suspicion of murder; charges against Sally's husband were soon dropped. He never ceased to support Sally's version of events. At Sally's trial in October 1999, an expert witness, paediatrician Roy Meadow, testified that the likelihood of the death of two children in these circumstances was 1 in 73 million: 'like backing an 80-1 shot at the Grand National four years running, and winning each time'. Sally was convicted and the conviction upheld on appeal. She was widely vilified as a child murderer. There was speculation in the media about the frustration of educated mothers who found themselves obliged to be at home with young children.

Aided by a sympathetic lawyer who distrusted the verdict, Sally's husband discovered that crucial medical evidence known to the prosecution had been withheld from the defence. In addition, the striking 1 in 73 million statistic was discredited. The Court of Appeal referred the case to the Criminal Cases Review Commission, and after three years in prison, Sally was released in January 2003. The Attorney General reviewed hundreds of other cases and three women accused or convicted on the testimony of the same paediatrician were exonerated.

Sally never got over her experience, suffering from personality change, profound grief and alcohol dependency. She died four years later, aged 42.

The miscarriage of justice here was to confuse a tragedy with a crime. That two tiny children should die was a profound tragedy – attributable to life, biology, fate or God, depending on your point of view. But somehow in this case the combined weight of medical research and legal procedure couldn't accept that tragedies happen. Tragedy had to be re-narrated as murder – even if it meant distorting the evidence, misusing statistics and withholding crucial information from the defence. The death of the two infant boys was unjust, in the sense that it would be natural to wish any prospective parent a smooth path through their children's upbringing and any infant child a healthy start to life; but in the narrow, forensic sense, it wasn't unjust at all: it was unlucky. The case is a warning that trying to turn every kind of sadness into a form of injustice is not merely psychologically and theologically mistaken, but can have major deleterious legal consequences.

If this was a case of finding a culprit when in reality no one was to blame, miscarriage of justice is perhaps more frequently associated with circumstances where the crime is evident for all to see but the wrong party has been identified as the perpetrator. Late on the evening of 21 November 1974 at Heysham, Lancashire, six men were arrested en route to the funeral of a Provisional IRA member who had recently been killed by his own bomb. Earlier that evening, 21 people had been killed and 182 injured at two pub bombings in Birmingham. Five of the men arrested had left Birmingham shortly before the bombs exploded. A forensic scientist maintained he was 99 per cent certain two of the men had traces of explosives on their hands. On 15 August 1975, they were sentenced to 21 life sentences.

It became clear that the six men had been subject to beatings and other forms of torture and intimidation at the hands of police and prison officer interrogators. These led four of the men to sign confession statements. Attempts to prosecute the officers involved failed and leave to appeal the convictions was not granted. In 1986, the journalist Chris Mullin published detailed arguments maintaining the men's innocence, together with claims of knowing the true perpetrators. The Court of Appeal ruled the original verdicts safe in 1988, but the campaign grew in momentum. At a second appeal in 1991, evidence of police malpractice, the discrediting of the four confessions and the invalidation of the forensic evidence was such that the Crown withdrew its case. In 2001, the six men each gained compensation of around £1 million. At the reopened inquests into the deaths of the 21 victims, on 22 March 2019, a convicted IRA bomber known as Witness O named the four men he claimed were genuinely responsible for the crime.[3]

In this case, the miscarriage of justice was to insist that, after a terrible crime, people must be held accountable – but to be less concerned that the right people be held responsible. To punish one person for the crime of another may assuage anger, grief and hurt; but it's not justice. In the arrest, charge and prosecution of the Birmingham Six there seems to have been an intense desire to punish, deter and eradicate terrorists – but insufficient commitment to ensure that the democratic

---

3 BBC, 'Birmingham pub bombings: "Men responsible" named by IRA bomber', *BBC News*, 22 March 2019, https://www.bbc.co.uk/news/uk-england-birmingham-47670167, accessed 26.12.2021.

values the authorities existed to uphold were embodied in the way they sought to uphold them. At least some of those bringing the men to trial must have been well aware that there was no solid basis for convicting them. Justice is not the serving-up of some plausible culprits to an angry public; it's the careful identification of the true perpetrators and the rigorous prosecution of them, by appropriate means and with the submission of compelling evidence. When the severity of the crime is matched by the inadequacy of the conviction, the wrong is not allayed, but multiplied.

But the miscarriage of justice can be of a third kind – when a crime has indeed been committed, but there is a conspiracy to deny it, plead misfortune and yet meanwhile blame the victim. At Hillsborough Stadium, Sheffield, on 15 April 1989, a fatal human crush at the start of the FA Cup semi-final between Liverpool and Nottingham Forest caused 97 deaths and 766 injuries. While the 1990 Taylor Report maintained the principal cause of the disaster was the failure of the South Yorkshire Police to control the crowd at the Liverpool fans' end, the inquests reached a verdict of accidental death, while the Director of Public Prosecutions found no reason to bring any individuals or institutions to trial. From the very first, the South Yorkshire Police and others with an interest in defaming the Liverpool supporters put about stories that it was their hooliganism and drunkenness, rather than negligence and mismanagement by the police, and the long-standing inadequate condition of the stadium, that constituted the true causes of the tragedy. Families of the victims failed to secure a second inquiry in 1997 and failed again in private prosecutions against senior police officers in 2000. The tide began to turn in 2012, when an independent panel highlighted the many forces that had combined to suppress the truth and opened a new round of inquests. In 2016, these inquests found that the supporters had been unlawfully killed due to gross negligence on the part of police and ambulance services and due to the poor design of the stadium; the supporters were not to blame. In 2017, six police officers were prosecuted; by 2021 all these prosecutions had failed. As a result, not one single police officer was finally held to account for the catastrophe. The Leader of the House of Commons, Jacob Rees-Mogg, described this on 27 May 2021 as 'the greatest scandal of British policing of our lifetimes'.[4]

This was not a simple miscarriage of justice. This was a failure on every level – personal, institutional, cultural, political, legal. There had been a series of near-catastrophes of a similar kind at the stadium. The licence for the stand in question had lapsed in 1981, but the stand was still in use. Four days after the disaster, *The Sun* newspaper carried the headline 'The Truth', under which it listed three claims: 'Some fans picked pockets of victims', 'Some fans urinated on the brave cops' and 'Some fans beat up PC giving kiss of life'. These slanders epitomized a culture in which police attempts to transfer culpability colluded with a widespread incapability to address the tragedy without a pre-existing narrative overshadowing the evidence. The truth is that, despite the families' 30-year quest for justice, many aspects of that pre-existing narrative continue to shape the way the events are remembered. In such a case, justice isn't limited to changing the results of a misguided inquest, or

---

4 BBC, 'Lack of Hillsborough accountability is a scandal, says minister', *BBC News*, 27 May 2021, https://www.bbc.co.uk/news/uk-england-merseyside-57266824, accessed 26.12.2021.

seeking to hold individuals to account, or even demanding a change of heart from those who conspired to misrepresent the victims; justice requires repentance and transformation on the part of individuals, institutions and cultural icons at every level of society.

The exposure of miscarriages of justice is not a statement of the failure of the justice system, but of the vital role of scrutiny in patrolling it. Justice may be subverted for a number of reasons: because its processes are used for cases that involve no crime, because the urge to find someone to blame outweighs the insistence that it should be the one truly to blame, because a rush to judgement forgets to regard a person as innocent until proven guilty, or because those indeed to blame succeed in diverting attention to other parties. Justice thus needs restraint as well as energy; passion can be a liability as much as an asset. Meanwhile, miscarriages of justice are not the only area where close scrutiny is needed: the cataloguing of human-rights violations and the exposure of corporate malpractice are two notable additional examples. Constant vigilance is demanding, unspectacular and ill-rewarded; but it is integral to justice.

PART 3

Correcting Injustice

Having explored the dimensions of constructive justice, this next part of the book considers corrective justice. I make no secret of the effort and commitment this involves. If one perceives those who establish the norms of justice as well intentioned, the quest to advance the cause of those who nonetheless experience injustice is a demanding one. If one accepts that not all of those norm-setters are well intentioned, and that some are exploitative, cruel and harsh, the task becomes even harder and more adversarial. So the chapters in this part concern struggle and organizing, which are ways to find power even in depleted circumstances. But the third chapter in this section also explores support and touches on the complexity and pitfalls of seeking to act justly.

7

Struggle

Good order sounds wonderful, but the truth is, it still doesn't constitute justice. The reason is that good order, as the name suggests, concentrates on order – and maintaining order, when that order is itself unjust, isn't justice. The justice of good order has little will and almost no capacity to redistribute power, and it's in unequal distribution of power that a great deal of injustice actually lies.

Imagine an immigrant child. His family doesn't speak good English. He finds his parents split up. His mother, with whom he lives, is seriously ill, so he has to become her carer. He also does the shopping, cooking and cleaning to an extent few children comprehend. These responsibilities fill his time and drain his energy. As a result, he does poorly at school, loses the opportunity to make the most of his talents and finds the doors to further education shut. No law has been broken, no culture of the rule of law has lapsed; but he has discovered, very young and very painfully, that good judgements and good order are only part of what justice involves. Likewise, if he grows up and there's a new government, and his residency status changes, he has little recourse to legal advocacy, whereas those against him have plenty. Again, no law has been broken. But the law has proved incapable of delivering justice.

A simple image is that of three people trying to look over a fence. One is tall and has no difficulty seeing, perhaps appreciating the fence as something to lean on to watch a game. Another is shorter and can only see part of the game, even on tiptoes. A third is shorter still and cannot see the game at all. If everyone is given a box to stand on, this may be called equality; but the tallest person doesn't need the box, while the shortest person still can't see over the fence. If the shortest person is given two boxes, and the tallest person none, this may be called equity. If the fence is removed by the shortest person aided by the middle-height person, we could call it liberation. Social justice seeks equity en route to liberation.[1] The illustration shows how justice isn't the same as equality. Instead, justice is the right judgement of how difference should be understood and cherished, rather than permitted to become an opportunity for exploitation. People invoke the term 'social justice' when they're especially concerned to affirm equal access to vital resources such as education, shelter, food and health care, and active participation in decision-making by those most vulnerable or excluded.

This is the point where people begin to talk of 'structural injustice'. Structural injustice highlights that, while some have ample opportunity to develop and exercise their capacities, others do not, and experience domination at the hands of exploiters or deprivation of the goods of life. Unlike conventional injustice, it does not require wrongful action or malicious intent on the part of an individual: it can come about, as in the situation of the immigrant child above, simply through the accepted

---

1 See Human Rights Careers, 'What does social justice mean?', *Human Rights Careers*, https://www.humanrightscareers.com/issues/what-does-social-justice-mean/, accessed 29.12.2021.

processes of a society. We can perceive three kinds of structural injustice.[2]

The first is impersonal: there is no guilty party. Instead, a whole swathe of people are caught up in a social process that leaves an individual experiencing domination or deprivation. An example would be a single mother whose landlord wishes to redevelop the property in which she lives. Her options to move are limited to nearby flats that are too expensive, inner-city locations that are too dangerous, and suburban properties that would require her to buy a car. Having bought a car, she then has no money for a deposit on a flat. She is at risk of homelessness, but it is hard to blame a specific landlord, politician, employer, lender or developer, and doing so won't change the situation.[3]

The second is complicit: there's no specific guilty party in bringing a situation about. Nonetheless, those with power have the capacity, and therefore responsibility, to effect significant change – yet choose not to do so. An example would be the international refugee crisis. In the face of oppression or instability in overseas countries, Western nations have sometimes supported one side, other times taken direct military action, sometimes imposed sanctions, or other times stayed well

---

2 These three are adapted from the three outlined in Maeve McKeown, *With Power Comes Responsibility: The Politics of Structural Injustice* (London: Bloomsbury, 2022). See also the very helpful Maeve McKeown, 'Structural injustice', *Philosophy Compass* 16/7 (July 2021), https://onlinelibrary.wiley.com/doi/10.1111/phc3.12757.

3 This is an abbreviation of a much-cited example in Iris Marion Young, *Responsibility for Justice* (Oxford: Oxford University Press, 2011), pp. 43–4. The popularity of the term 'structural injustice' is significantly due to the influence of Young's work.

away. If such action or inaction has not produced the desired outcome, a common result is an increasing flow of refugees. Ideally, refugees can be accommodated elsewhere in their own country or supported in a neighbouring country. If those Western policies, even though wholly or largely well-intentioned, have failed, Western governments have a responsibility to address the outcomes of that failed policy by engaging with refugees on their own borders – because they have the capacity to do so, and the refugees have no alternative.

The third is intentional: this is where there is indeed a guilty party. A situation has come about because influential bodies have lobbied government for advantages (often with a personal or political payback to individual politicians) and often threatened them with taking their business elsewhere, but those advantages have inflicted domination or deprivation on others. One example is sweatshop labour. Developing world economies tolerate clothing factories that exploit staff members in hours worked, pay earned, compromised health and safety and violent supervision. But these are not simply the fault of factory owners, or even negligent regimes. There's a global market for garments, and developing nations compete with one another to offer advantageous conditions in which multinational corporations can operate.[4]

This threefold distinction has a number of helpful applications. It begins to break down the powerlessness of the struggle against injustice by assisting activists in identifying which battles to fight. The crucial move is to distinguish between who caused the problem, if anyone, and who is best placed, or obliged, to address it. A simplistic view might assume that every injustice

4 This example also comes from Young, *Responsibility for Justice*, pp. 131–2.

has a personal cause – either one's own shortcomings or the malice of another – and one must either sort it out oneself or seek redress from the perpetrator. This more sophisticated three-dimensional perspective helps explain why seeking a personal cause is often fruitless and why the fact that no one is available to take the blame is not a good reason for resultant inaction.

Take the example of the legacy of slavery. It's obviously a category-three issue – the transatlantic slave trade and the practice of slavery were without question brought about by individuals for their own economic and social advantage and at every stage directly resulted in domination and deprivation among the slaves. But because slavery in the United States ended 150 years ago, some would rather treat it as a category-one issue – something for which no one living is responsible and thus 'just one of those things'. The point to highlight is that because of the subsequent legacy of segregation and the abiding post-civil rights culture of oppression towards African Americans, it's a long way from being a category-one issue. Today it's a mixture of a category-two and category-three issue. The work is to appreciate the difference between the two.

Here's what a category-two treatment looks like: 'The point is not about seeking a culprit centuries ago. The point is to see how social processes in housing, policing, education and public services right now are perpetuating a culture of oppression towards African Americans, and how this is a social system that involves every citizen of this nation, and particularly advantages some. We can explore the history if it helps you see how intricately and profoundly the legacy of subjugation has infiltrated every aspect of US society; but the emphasis needs to be on the present and the future, and on what must be done to ensure every African American finds genuine opportunity, real security, dynamic agency and true belonging in this society, so the statement that "Black lives matter" is not a defiant assertion in the face of injustice but a proud description of a lived reality.' A category-three treatment, by contrast, would be more concerned to diagnose the way understandings of dominance have pervaded the American narrative from the first settler times, more invested in demanding history be addressed in relation to reparations and statues and more focused on identifying the descendants and beneficiaries of the perpetrators as the ones on whom responsibility now lies for changing the power relations and social outcomes.

The issue here is not about determining whether category two or category three is the right designation in all circumstances. It's about recognizing the three different kinds of structural injustice and realizing that there might be different contexts in which one applies more helpfully than the others, as well as being able to use the threefold distinction to recognize where the wrong kind of structural injustice is being invoked.

Another setting where the threefold distinction is helpful is the climate emergency. Structural injustice is about recognizing that there are kinds of injustice that don't necessarily have a personal perpetrator – but where not being part of the problem doesn't take away responsibility for being part of the solution. Today we have a new version of this kind of justice: it's doing justice to future generations. Most of the actions that are destroying the earth as a habitat for humans and many other creatures constitute no crime, and the people who will suffer most don't yet exist; but it's hard to deny that the effects of climate change are profoundly unjust. The threefold definition of structural injustice is again helpful here: there's an impersonal, category-one quality to where you happen to live in the world, and to what extent you are therefore most vulnerable to the more pressing extremes of the climate emergency; there's an intentional, category-three character to those activities that are most damaging to our global future, and are knowingly carried out by those who could put their energies and commercial activities elsewhere – particularly those who perpetuate climate scepticism; and there's a complicit element to almost all human activity now that the facts about the crisis are widely known.

In which ways, for example, are the loggers who cut down the Amazon rainforest examples of category two – caught up in matters that are no one's fault, but that their government must resolve, and quickly? Or in which ways is this a case of category three, individuals being caught up in a system that benefits those whose faces we never see? Hard as it is to avoid anger and finger-pointing, the centre of the solution to the climate debate today is to explore the full dimensions of what category two entails: not to apportion blame, even less to shrug shoulders and say little can be done, but to define and implement specific actions that individuals and institutions at every level of society can take to address an urgent, global crisis. The second category stands out because it affirms a collective, empowering and motivating 'we', rather than taking refuge, as the others tend to, in a sympathetic, impervious or accusatory 'you'.

The crucial move in relation to structural injustice is to divest category one of its debilitating, demotivating power and to establish how most dimensions of category one can be transferred, accurately and patiently, into categories two or three. The principal difference between category one and the two subsequent categories is not identifying who's to blame, but building a coalition of who's going to do something about it. The danger that lies in the language of structural injustice is that it polarizes responses. Some assume that there are grand-scale things for which no one is to blame, that a term such as 'structural' is inherently divisive, since it points the finger at those at the top of any identified structure, and that we should instead concentrate on individual acts of wrongdoing: in other words, that category one is the only category. Others assume that the task is to highlight the exploiters and shame them into making the necessary changes themselves: in other words, that category three is the only category and that all injustice lies at the feet of a particular social class. There are certainly things that belong in category three, but the most productive approach is to converge on the second category – to acknowledge that all, or almost all, are complicit, and to set about finding roles each can take up in making things better.

Struggle is the kind of justice to which those who campaign for justice are usually committed. Struggle most often identifies repeated, endemic, daily injustice, in a place or pattern or profession, which authorities are loath to acknowledge and the wider public reluctant to notice, but which marching, tweeting, protesting, picketing, boycotting or resisting at the point of occurrence can expose to the light of publicity, whence the wind of change may in time become hard to withstand. Struggle sometimes applies to conventional justice: the quests described in the previous chapter of the Hillsborough families, or the supporters of the Birmingham Six, or Rob Bilott and his battle with DuPont are all kinds of struggle. But struggle most characteristically occupies the territory of category three above.

In this sense, struggle tends to follow these or similar stages. A person or a number of people among an oppressed group realize this is not just a category-one problem but most likely a category-three problem – their plight is the direct outcome of operations carried out according to the design of influential individuals or groups and only putting pressure on them will bring it to an end. Then, in many cases, supporters are found from beyond the oppressed group. These supporters can play two useful roles: they can help persuade a larger number of the oppressed group that their situation isn't inevitable and can be resolved, and they can stir the imagination, conscience and energy of members of the wider society to share and express concern.

At this point, several kinds of conflict emerge: between victims who believe change is achievable and near, and those who fear making things worse; between victims and supporters who advocate direct action, and those who want to use persuasion and influence key actors behind the scenes; between supporters who are committed to being in an ancillary role only in a movement directed by victims, and supporters who believe they sometimes know better than victims how oppression works or how to achieve change; and between the wider public who shrink from direct action, and those who are aware that oppressors seldom give up without a fight. Many liberation movements are so divided within themselves about causes, methods and partners that they exhaust their energy without confronting the oppressor. Hence the biting humour in the Monty Python film *Life of Brian* when it portrays the antagonism between the Judean People's Front and the People's Front of Judea. What this moment reveals is that, however simple the issue might be, however obvious the task might seem, a struggle for justice is *always* a coalition, because there is always a range of stakeholders, always a dispute about methods, always a diversity of diagnoses of the real problem, always a debate about who is truly part of the movement and always a difference of view about what constitutes success. Struggle attracts the headstrong, the passionate and the impatient – but it seldom succeeds unless it finds a place for all temperaments and all skills.

Thus, the Anti-Apartheid Movement began in London in 1959 by boycotting South African goods. After the Sharpeville Massacre in 1960, the movement expanded its aims towards the economic and cultural isolation of South Africa. It had notable successes when South Africa was forced to leave the Commonwealth in 1961 and was suspended from the Olympics in 1964. However, Western governments remained opposed to the campaign, purportedly because those it would mainly hurt would be the most vulnerable in South Africa, whom the West was keen to uphold. The campaign morphed into the Free Nelson Mandela movement, which drew huge numbers through its use of music festivals: thus, a concert at Wembley Stadium in 1988 attracted a crowd of 100,000 and a global television audience of 600 million. But in 1990, once Mandela was free, the campaign faced its biggest challenge: when had it achieved its goal? Some abandoned the quest. Others waited till free elections in 1994. Others thereafter formed Action for Southern Africa. The story illustrates all the attractions and pitfalls of such a struggle – not least, that it's easier to gather momentum to oppose an evil than to uphold a good.

That is the challenge for the climate-justice agenda, arguably the definitive global struggle of our time. Climate justice refers to the prospect of a safe climate for future generations, a fair and equal distribution of the global carbon budget between countries and, within countries, of economies where people's housing, transport and energy needs are met, while the burden falls proportionately on those most able to pay. These goals offer a positive understanding of justice, but they're not as compelling as the notion of rebellion against extinction. Yet every struggle against injustice must eventually turn into something more complex, subtle and patient: a quest for justice.

8

Organize

The second element of asserting justice is to organize. Organizing confronts those who say they genuinely want to bring about change with the blunt question: 'Are you prepared to adopt the tactics likely to achieve that change?' Organizing is about power. It recognizes that if you let others have power, you can't complain or be surprised if they walk all over you. It's therefore committed to taking up legitimate and appropriate kinds of power. Power can, without doubt, be used for ill; but it can also be used for good. There's no especial sanctity about being powerless. Organizing is also about using tension for purposeful ends. It renounces the lazy or sentimental notion of a life without tension. It perceives that bringing latent tension to the surface is often the best, or only, way to address injustice. But tension is only ever a means to the end of justice. It's a tactic used by those who understand that without justice, there can never be genuine peace.

We may think of three kinds of organizing: where you have individual power, but it's a new thought to activate that power for the cause of justice; where you have little individual power, but can organize to a collective goal; and where you have significant collective interaction, practice and trust, but you'd not previously recognized its capacity to be used for wider ends.

An example of the first kind, the turning of individual power to the cause of justice, is shareholder action. Shareholder activists purchase a minority stake in a publicly traded company and then use their rights as shareholders to make that company behave better internally towards its employees or externally in relation to its customers, clients or social impact. Whereas shareholding is conventionally understood as a way of gaining income through a company's annual profit dividend, activism changes the nature of this relationship from passive to active and seeks to make the company a force for social good, or justice – either by ceasing to do harm, or by taking leadership in setting a healthy example.

The most direct way to do this is by exercising voting rights at a company's annual meeting. Shareholders may declare that they are only willing to support directors who, for example, will pursue a just approach to the climate emergency. Thus, they may bring a proposal for a company's recruitment policy to be voted on by other shareholders at such a meeting. But there are other tactics. A shareholder may use inside knowledge to threaten litigation against a company, or to generate support through a media campaign. In 2016, a class action was brought against the Exxon Mobil Corporation, maintaining that it had made false and misleading statements relating to the impact of climate change on its business; namely, that it had significantly overstated the value of its oil reserves and artificially inflated the company's value. This was the first shareholder-led lawsuit alleging failure to disclose climate risk. Climate justice is by no means the only issue liable to action of this kind: shareholders may seek disinvestment from an authoritarian regime in a developing country, or the cessation of partnership with factories in a state notorious for condoning sweatshop conditions. What's happening here is a subtle reversal of shareholder and board member. Conventionally, the board is looking to the long-term well-being of the organization, while the shareholder is focused on short-term financial gain. But the shareholder activist leapfrogs the board by pointing to a much wider sense of well-being and a much stronger awareness of social impact, thus transforming the dynamic entirely, often leaving the board confused and defensive.

One initiative targeted hedge fund companies. On 20 April 2021, 140 racial-justice leaders published an open letter to asset managers as a full-page *Financial Times* advert.[1] They accused financial institutions of 'continuing to eschew accountability or disruption to the status quo that perpetuates racism and its harms'. As examples, the letter highlighted the prevalence of all-white boards, discriminatory corporate behaviour, such as financing pipelines that run through Indigenous lands, and funnelling corporate donations to legislators who support voter suppression efforts. In addition, the letter demanded equitable workplace practices and an end to customer discrimination, algorithmic bias and community surveillance. Anything less would constitute continued complicity in systemic racism. The letter was specifically aimed at three corporations that held 25 per cent of voting shares in the leading US companies but had made almost no steps in the wake of the Black Lives Matter protests to rectify racist company practices. The tactic was designed to eradicate the middle, non-committal

---

1 Majority Action, 'Letter to asset managers', *Majority Action*, https://www.racialjustice.majorityaction.us/letter-to-asset-managers, accessed 27.12.2021.

ground between actively supporting anti-racist policies and being identified as a racist company.[2]

The second kind of organizing refers to those who have little individual power but can organize to a collective goal. Rather than lament its deficits, this kind of organizing begins by assessing its assets. The first of these is relationship. Relationship is power. Any struggle is preceded by one-to-one meetings and careful listening – both to learn, and to harness the trust and engagement of stakeholders. There's a sober recognition that injustice won't go away on its own. What makes people act is their interest – and their passion. The point where these two interact, and are shared by a community, provides the dynamism for action. Thus a movement, while perhaps short on physical or economic power, can cultivate relational power as citizens combine to address common concerns and issues that beset their neighbourhood. This relational quality enables those of profoundly different backgrounds to face disagreement as friends, rather than as strangers. To build a movement takes leaders – those identified in face-to-face meetings and trained in collective, imaginative action, who listen to, work alongside and raise up the gifts of others. The organizer Al Giordano puts it like this:

> If it doesn't involve knocking on doors, making phone calls or otherwise proactively communicating with people demographically different [from] you, it's not organising. If it doesn't involve face-to-face building

---

2 A subsequent article noted not much change had resulted: Attracta Mooney and Madison Darbyshire, 'Race and finance: asset managers fail to walk the walk', *Financial Times*, 28 December 2021, https://www.ft.com/content/59d8f7c4-cc9e-41 a4-b739-c43c4195d592, accessed 22.1.2022.

of relationships, teams, chains of command, and, day-by-day, clear goals to measure its progress and effectiveness, it's not organising. If it happens only on the internet, that's not organising either.[3]

Organizers see their work as different from mobilizing. Organizing has a greater concern for the people with whom it is engaging. It perceives mobilizing as simply using people to become active in a campaign, while having no other genuine concern for them. By contrast, organizers take time to develop the capacity of participants as leaders and to make relational connections, seeing both as not just means to an end, but as ends in themselves. Justice isn't simply the demolition of obstacles – it's the building of community through the unleashing of the power latent in that community. Organizing is a constantly rolling snowball of experience, digested by reflection, and sometimes research, into new, creative action, leading to new experience, generating new relationships and identifying new leaders. The momentum of this spiral is a characteristic of organizing. So is the way impetus gained by a small success leads to growing confidence, in turn yielding even greater successes. Thus, justice becomes a never-completed but always-inspiring goal, and the practices that line the way to justice become as significant as justice itself. These practices develop a shared narrative, and a shared narrative is a power that only relationship can bring.

Beyond justice, organizing is fundamentally about power. Organizers speak about their opposition to

---

3 Quoted in James Whelan and Jason MacLeod, 'What is community organising?', *The Commons Social Change Library*, https://commonslibrary.org/what-is-community-organising/, accessed 27.12.2021.

power-over, domination and exploitation; about their awakening of individuals' latent *power-from-within*, the belief, skills and knowledge that give them true agency; about building capacity to exercise *power-with*, to take collective action.[4] Organizers distinguish three kinds of activity: (a) Social-movement organizing gathers energy around a major issue such as minimum wage, refugee rights or prison reform. It builds a coalition, holding together diverse interests for a temporary campaign. (b) Neighbourhood organizing is about local issues. Its work is as much about increasing individuals' engagement with and sense of their local community as about confronting and negotiating with those who hold power in government or business boardrooms. (c) Broad-based organizing focuses on developing active citizenship and grassroots democracy. Its members are value-based organizations like churches, other faith groups and trade unions, and those members make an annual subscription to pay for organizers. These umbrella organizations are generally affiliated, in the UK, to the Industrial Areas Foundation. They work through listening campaigns and use tactics like citizens' assemblies, where decision-makers can be held publicly to account.

The history of the campaign for a living wage in the UK illustrates a combination of social-movement and broad-based organizing.[5] The Nonconformist textile industrialist and Liberal MP Mark Oldroyd made the first reasoned argument for a living wage in 1894, proposing decent surroundings, sufficient leisure and respectable income

---

4 See Whelan and MacLeod, 'What is community organising?'

5 For putting this campaign in a wider historical context, see 'A short history of the living wage in the UK', *Queen Mary University of London*, https://www.qmul.ac.uk/geog/livingwage/history/, accessed 14.3.2022.

as vital to enable a person to work effectively and be a good citizen, thus expressing their moral worth. Since then, arguments have always blended human dignity with greater workplace efficiency and greater rates of consumption. The emergence of the welfare state, with its provision of education, health, housing and pensions, was accompanied by the practice of collective bargaining. This ensured that widespread poverty did not re-emerge until the 1970s. The 1998 National Minimum Wage Act established a Low Pay Commission that, for the first time, set a national minimum wage. But this was never set high enough to address in-work poverty. Inspired by the success of Baltimoreans United in Leadership Development, which had spawned a hundred imitators in the United States, London Citizens launched a broad-based organizing campaign for a living wage in 2001. Its arguments were holistic – noting effects on health outcomes, educational achievement, parenting, family life and civility. A signal achievement was ensuring all new jobs at the 2012 Olympic site in Stratford would be living wage. By creating a Living Wage Week each November, the Living Wage Foundation has been able to focus media attention, announce the new rate for the forthcoming year and highlight participating organizations.

The third area of organizing refers to when you have significant collective interaction, practice and trust, but had not previously recognized its capacity to be used for wider ends. This refers to the church. The church's power to act justly is seldom realized. It has a profound tradition, much of it rooted in the call of the Old Testament prophets for people to love their neighbour as a way of demonstrating faithfulness to God, and summed up in the announcement of Mary to Elizabeth that, 'He has brought down the powerful from their thrones, and lifted up the lowly; he has filled the hungry with good things, and sent the rich away empty.'[6] It has an enormous network of local congregations in every community, with a vast voluntary base of people willing to give in time and money to issues that embody God's love for the outcast and that promise to challenge and change the unjust social structures. And it has extraordinarily good connections with the ruling elites in most countries, particularly the Western democracies, where decisions with global impact are made. The secret is to identify where these three capacities converge.

Such an instance was the Jubilee 2000 campaign for debt relief. This was by no means a church-only or church-dominated campaign; but it would be fair to call it a church-animated one. It originated from the description of the jubilee year in Leviticus 25.8–22 and the according notion that debts should not be maintained indefinitely but should be cancelled every fiftieth year. The campaign was founded in the early 1990s by a retired academic, Martin Dent, to link the notion of jubilee to the upcoming millennium. The movement identified highly indebted poor countries in Africa, Latin America, Asia and the Middle East, and highlighted how falling behind with debt repayments to richer countries meant these highly indebted countries were paying out more to service (not even eradicate) the debt than they were receiving in aid. Thus, sustaining the debt was impoverishing developing countries – and, to use an emotive phrase, literally killing their children by diverting money that could have been spent on poverty relief. Filling the space created by the end of the

---

6 Luke 1.52–53.

Cold War, pressure groups in the West capitalized on the opportunity to bring to the surface issues long suppressed – among them land mines, diamonds and child labour. Jubilee 2000 picked up on this momentum.

The campaign began with congregations and youth groups in the UK. By the late 1990s, with the imaginative direction of Ann Pettifor, this had expanded to church leaders and celebrities, including Bono, the Pope and, remarkably, the American ultra conservative Pat Robertson; it also reached government leaders, such as Chancellor of the Exchequer Gordon Brown and Prime Minister Tony Blair. Churches and other groups turned it into a mass movement: there was a huge programme of letter-writing and lobbying; 50,000 people encircled the G8 summit in Birmingham in 1998 and 30,000 the Cologne G7 summit a year later. While the campaign undoubtedly gained more traction in the two countries, Britain and Canada, that were owed the least, and had rather less appeal in the two, France and Japan, that were owed the most, the outcomes were very positive: in 2000, the US Congress committed $769 million to bilateral and multilateral debt relief and overall, £100 billion of debt owed by 35 of the world's poorest countries was cancelled.

This was a highly effective convergence of the church's three forms of power. It was a perfect example of a long-held tradition, the jubilee, being introduced into the public sphere, which resonated with common ideas of fairness, other movements for a rebalancing of the global power structure and a succinctly articulated demand. It was an extraordinarily successful galvanizing of the will and energy of local congregations, enormous numbers of which organized around its simple message and straightforward methods. And it was an almost uniquely positive case of the church using its strong connections in public life and civil society to find celebrity advocates and persuade powerful politicians. Of course, issues were simplified, aims not wholly met and unfinished business remains; but immense good was nonetheless done, and the identification of the church with the cause of justice unequivocally affirmed.

9

Support

The paradox of seeking justice is that, by advocating and agitating around an issue or denouncing or demonstrating against a wrong, you could, without realizing, be reaffirming a deeper problem than the one against which you think you're campaigning. That problem is that you still end up as the centre of the story. The phrase 'It's not about you' functions on many levels. It can refer to changing the story of international development away from one in which Westerners have all the resources and Africans have all the need. It can describe discouraging the way white people can appropriate the story of racial justice. It can involve challenging a 'white saviour' configuration of any situation of cross-cultural or international inequality. What these examples have in common is a single word: 'decentring'. Decentring means both humbly realizing that you might not be the key actor in advancing justice, and also carefully identifying, usually with the help and decisive judgement of those who *are* the key actors, where your energies, skills, contacts, experience and financial support may nonetheless prove useful.

One of the most vexed issues is how to address the enormous difference in health, security and life outcomes between citizens of the West and those of the developing world. Towards the end of the Second World War, the World Bank and International Monetary Fund were created to address structural inequality and to finance the transformation of developing-world economies. Meanwhile, the creation of the welfare state in the UK began to turn the eyes of charitable donors from the home front to needs overseas. This was the climate in which great overseas agencies like Oxfam and Christian Aid were born. Many of the questions that surround their work were there from the beginning. Was governmental overseas aid a form of charity, or enlightened self-interest? While successive governments tied aid to spending on UK exports and adoption of Western ideologies (notably backing the West in the Cold War), public perception continued to dwell on 'charitable' issues such as whether support was more needed at home. Were independent charities the best channels for international aid, given their extensive local networks and ongoing relationships with grassroots agents, in contrast to the government's dependence on senior officials – and consequent liability to dissipating investment through endemic corruption? Governments were understandably reluctant to subcontract control over aid in this manner, even if the outcomes in doing so were invariably better. Most significantly, did the whole notion of international aid, and the rhetoric generated to fund it, reinforce perhaps the basic problem – that of Western perception of its own superiority, and difficulty in comprehending a 'solution' that did not characterize itself as a saviour? Eye-catching events like the Live Aid concert at Wembley in 1985 mobilized a large public, but at the cost of characterizing the issues as ones that Africa had foolishly created, and the West could compassionately and intelligently solve.

In recent decades, the ethos of overseas aid, certainly in the charitable sector, has focused more explicitly on narratives that affirm partnership between the different actors: local farmers and businesspeople, local government officials, advisers and network coordinators from the aid agencies, individual donors in the West, Western governmental international development investment and local government oversight. Good outcomes in such a story are best advanced by toning down the aspiration for turning injustice into justice to a more modest building of momentum for healthy local economies and enhanced community well-being resulting from local people's greater ability to feel agency, create income, strengthen community and find solutions to their problems locally. While disaster relief is sometimes appropriate, making the child starving in a famine or family deprived of their home by flooding the emblem of overseas aid diminishes the structural issues and takes dignity away from recipients. The remarkable success of having the eight Millennium Development Goals agreed by every country in the world in 2000 has shaped a new culture, and the 17 Sustainable Development Goals adopted in 2015 make clear that the real tasks are ones that require contributions from every participant.[1]

To act justly in international aid is not a simple matter of taking from one's own abundance and instantly rectifying another's scarcity. Such a view – reducing structural inequality to a face-to-face transaction, laying the guilt on the one party and assuming the humble

---

1 An extraordinarily helpful survey of issues in international development is *Freedom from Oppression: Government Communication on Swedish Democracy Support* (Stockholm: Ministry for Foreign Affairs, 2007) available at https://www.government. se/contentassets/f09539l9d05242058600be5676d4b1c9/com munication-on-democracy-support-2008-comm.-20080911, accessed 5.1.2022.

gratitude of the other – is not just simplistic and inaccur-
ate. More seriously, it's counterproductive, reinforcing
the harmful stereotype that people in one part of the
world are feckless and cursed, while those in another
part are productive and magnanimous. Instead, acting
justly is about developing a number of ways to invest
in a common future. It's about recognizing and affirming (in a way few do) the enormous achievements of
international aid since the Second World War and the
number of people no longer facing extreme poverty.
And it's about anticipating a world where the culture,
habits and assumptions of the West cease to dominate,
manipulate and undermine the rest of the world, but
where respective parties will one day become true partners. One of the paradoxical successes of international
aid is the way China and India, once recipients of aid,
are now becoming more powerful than the Western
nations that once assisted them. This is a remarkable
success – though seldom portrayed as one.

The most practical defence of international aid is as
an alternative to war. War is the most 'centred' way
of approaching difference. The sceptic could be per-
suaded into investing in international aid by an advocate
demonstrating the cost of war, the proportionate success
of war, the cost of aid and the proportionate success of
aid. The figures speak for themselves. War is invariably
defended as a last resort; but seldom have the earlier
resorts, notably aid, been fully explored when the
political temperature was milder.

A second area where decentring is part of acting
justly is around the notion of being an ally. Being an
ally involves recognizing that the story is often, perhaps
usually, not about you. You may be a bystander in an
injustice that is being inflicted on someone else. But that

awareness need not lead to your walking away to mind your own business. On the contrary, there are several things you can constructively do, the most important of which is not to make yourself the centre of the story.

Allyship is fraught with potential for centring. 'Centring is a clear indication that you are not listening to understand, but rather listening to reply.'[2] The desire to ground another's plight in one's own experience is invariably not solidarity, but a subtle form of vacuuming their energy and imposing one's own: 'Our painful experiences may be valid, but when they're used as a tool to invalidate someone else's experience, they become erasure.' Good indications include whether the effect is to turn attention to oneself in a space that is not one's own, to alleviate guilt by displaying one's own struggles, even if irrelevant, changing the subject of the conversation, and using the word 'I' to prioritize one's own agency and validity. The motivation for centring is less likely to be narcissism than a desire for comfort in the face of deeply troubling testimony, but 'Change must not be contingent on comfort – because our comfort zones are toxic if they systemically hold no comfort for others.' Even the apparently innocent question, 'What can I do?' can be a form of centring, if it discloses an assumption that this is the most significant issue at stake and the principal one for others to address on one's behalf. The habit of centring is not simply a matter of conversational etiquette: because the issue of racism is so much about one social group's fear of no longer being

---

2 The quotations in this paragraph come from Emily Torres, 'What it means to center ourselves in conversation – and how to practice decentering instead', *The Good Trade*, https://www.thegoodtrade.com/features/decentering-yourself, accessed 29.12.2021.

the centre of the story, it is a route into the psychological heart of the whole problem.

An ally is a person who typically is unlikely to be the subject of injustice, who nonetheless explicitly stands beside those who are much more likely to be, so as to become a collaborator in reducing and eventually eliminating the almost routine discrimination and prejudice that often together constitute widespread injustice.[3] Becoming an ally begins with (1) seeking one's own education: not by expecting those subject to injustice to testify, which would put the burden on someone else, but by reading, watching and listening to the ample testimony already available. This should lead not only to understanding the history and invariably systemic nature of injustice, but also how common and habitually unquestioned behaviours embody and perpetuate it. A further step for allies is (2) to recognize their own social location: in particular, the comfort, advantage and success that's based not on merit, but on a loading of the dice that disproportionately bestows more opportunity, resources and power on some than on others; this is sometimes known as privilege. Having made such steps, an ally can (3) actively seek a trusted relationship across barriers such as race, class, gender, sexuality or disability within which to receive constructive criticism of their behaviour, and at the same time offer support and concern.

Thereafter being an ally is largely about (4) action that accelerates change on relational, institutional and

---

3 Among a great many articles on this theme, see for example Tsedale M. Melaku, Angie Beeman, David G. Smith and W. Brad Johnson, 'Be a better ally', *Harvard Business Review Magazine* (November–December 2020), https://hbr.org/2020/11/be-a-better-ally, accessed 21.1.2022.

societal levels. This can be proactive or reactive. Pro-active intervention is the use of power to make something happen that otherwise would have been overlooked. This could mean ensuring a diversity of perspectives are in the room at a meeting, that diverse voices are not just present but genuinely heard, and that those who find themselves alone in their identity are not expected to speak for every other under-represented identity. It could also mean advocating for a person to be given an opportunity that might not otherwise surface, and mentoring them so they can capitalize on openings they may hesitate to pursue. Reactive intervention means calling out unjust actions at the moment they happen, rather than waiting to sympathize later, or challenging in private, even when those subject to injustice are not present; thus accepting the risk that one's own judge-ments will be subject to scrutiny and criticism.

Being an ally is fraught with potential pitfalls. When it is a genuine 'working with' relationship, where each party yokes their respective talents and powers in ways that enhance the dignity of each, it can be a stirring and transformative process. If it becomes 'working for' advocacy, detached from any such relationship, it can share the dangers of all such interventions.[4] That is, it can become a virtue-signalling exercise rather than a sincere process of humility, learning and growth. It can use people rather than truly appreciate, enjoy and be accountable to them. If, for example, a person from a certain social group is murdered, a campaign ostensibly 'for' them, and the issues their death is taken to high-light, can spiral far beyond and well outside the actual

---

4 For extensive reflection on working for, working with, being with and being for, see my book, *A Nazareth Manifesto: Being with God* (Oxford: Wiley-Blackwell, 2015).

circumstances of their death, their own commitments in life or the wishes of their family and friends, and thereby not appropriately 'centre' or honour them at all. Being an ally means continuing to check in with and respect those one is seeking to support, rather than using that support as a platform for advancing one's own profile or agenda.

For some, the whole notion of allyship is fatally flawed, because it decentres the one who should be centred. James Baldwin describes the experience of being an African American as 'to be in a rage almost all the time'; hence, 'the first problem is how to control that rage so that it won't destroy you.' Baldwin describes how that rage is exacerbated by 'the most extraordinary and criminal indifference ... of most white people in this country'.[5] Focusing on 'what white people should do' is yet again to decentre the person on whom attention should focus. Austin Channing Brown describes the experience of reading Audre Lorde's transformative words. Speaking of a woman's anger, Lorde says, 'Focused with precision, [anger] can become a powerful source of energy serving progress and change ... Anger expressed and translated into action in the service of our vision and our future is a liberating and strengthening act of clarification.' Brown comments, 'Anger is not inherently destructive. My anger can be a force for good. My anger can be creative and imaginative, seeing a better world that doesn't yet exist.'[6] Here is a story that has found its true centre.

---

5 Quoted in Austin Channing Brown, *I'm Still Here: Black Dignity in a World Made for Whiteness* (London: Virago, 2020), p. 119.

6 Brown, *I'm Still Here*, pp. 125–6. See also 'Audre Lorde, "The uses of anger: women responding to racism"' (Original speech, 1981), *Blackpast*, 12 August 2012, https://www.black

Brené Brown seeks to steer a middle path as she help-fully distinguishes between guilt that may be constructive and shame that never is. Guilt involves 'holding some-thing we've done or failed to do up against our values, and feeling psychological discomfort'. Shame is the 'painful feeling or experience of believing that we are flawed and therefore unworthy of love and belonging'. Guilt is about what we've done; shame about what we are. Robin DiAngelo offers proposals to countering shame responses. She speaks of cultivating gratitude and humility, not trying to rationalize; listening and reflect-ing rather than withdrawing; and seeking to be told the truth about one's own blind spots. Elaine Enns and Ched Myers, considering what it means to be a settler among indigenous peoples, speak of developing healthy guilt that recognizes one's entanglement, yielding neither to shaming or blaming of self or others, and cultivating responsibility, restorative solidarity and reparation.[7]

The examples of international development and ally-ship in the face of another's daily experience of injustice demonstrate an abiding paradox in seeking justice: that apparently selfless efforts on behalf of another may prove to mask a subtle form of self-assertion and thus replicate or multiply the injustice rather than alleviate it.

---

past.org/african-american-history/speeches-african-american-history/1981-audre-lorde-uses-anger-women-responding-rac ism/, accessed 22.1.2022.

7 Brené Brown, 'Shame vs guilt', *Brené Brown*, 15 January 2013, https://brenebrown.com/articles/2013/01/15/shame-v-guilt/. Robin DiAngelo, *White Fragility: Why it's so Hard for White People to Talk About Racism* (Boston, MA: Beacon Press, 2018), pp. 141–2; Elaine Enns and Ched Myers, *Healing Haunted Histories: A Settler Discipleship of Decolonization* (Eugene, OR: Cascade Books, 2021), pp. 225–6. Enns and Myers are an excellent guide through this highly contested area.

From within the Christian tradition, Howard Thurman addresses this pitfall in a creative way by arguing that the circumstances of Christ's life provide a normative context for all Christian efforts towards justice. In his book *Jesus and the Disinherited*, Thurman argues that Christianity is originally and fundamentally directed towards those who stand 'with their backs against the wall'.[8] By using this phrase, Thurman not only, at a stroke, decentres all contemporary quests for justice, but highlights the significance of the African American experience under segregation as corresponding in many respects to the experience of Roman occupation in first-century Palestine. Thurman points out that Jesus was a poor Jew, a member of a minority group in the midst of a larger dominant and controlling group. The life of first-century Jews, Thurman insists, was dominated by their attitude towards Rome. 'Was any attitude possible that would be morally tolerable and at the same time preserve a basic self-esteem – without which life could not possibly have any meaning?'[9] In other words, how is survival possible? Thurman proposes this as the definitive context from which to seek justice.

Thurman goes on to examine Jesus' ministry by setting it alongside the alternative approaches to Roman occupation in the first century. Thurman notes the choice between non-resistance, pursued in different ways by Sadducees and Pharisees, and resistance, pursued violently by Zealots and non-violently by Jesus. Thurman highlights Jesus' phrase 'the kingdom of heaven is within you' and takes this to mean that we gain power by real-

---

8 Howard Thurman, *Jesus and the Disinherited* (Nashville, TN: Abingdon-Cokesbury Press, 1949; reprinted Boston, MA: Beacon Press, 1996), p. 3.

9 Thurman, *Jesus and the Disinherited*, p. 12.

izing it is our reaction to things that determines their ability to exercise power over us. Thurman concludes in ringing tones:

> The basic fact is that Christianity as it was born in the mind of this Jewish teacher and thinker appears as a technique of survival for the oppressed. That it became, through the intervening years, a religion of the powerful and the dominant, used sometimes as an instrument of oppression, must not tempt us into believing that it was thus in the mind and life of Jesus.[10]

What Thurman offers is a route to a profound and wholesale recentring of what it means to seek justice. The normative context is that of the group whose survival is in jeopardy – and not of any individual, group or state wishing to support or assist it. The normative activities are those that enable that group to survive with its integrity and identity intact – not the activities of those eager to rescue it. The normative mode of engagement is non-violent resistance – not violent overthrow or passive endurance. This is a deeply theological portrayal of justice. The reason why the African American experience is so significant today or why the situation of a trans person is such a key illustration of what justice means is because these contexts bear strong similarities to the context of a Jew in first-century Palestine: constantly under threat, perpetually seeking an identity and integrity not defined by the oppressive forces dominating society, longing, like Jesus, to find a path of non-violent resistance in the face of temptations to withdraw, violently oppose or passively accept the status quo.

---

10 Thurman, *Jesus and the Disinherited*, p. 18.

Thurman perceptively describes the three conditions into which the victim of oppression can descend. Violence and the permanent threat of violence produce *fear* – which can only be addressed by the Christian conviction that, as a child of God, they have an identity and worth beyond any damage inflicted by another.

Fear, then, becomes the safety device with which the oppressed surround themselves in order to give some measure of protection from complete nervous collapse. How do they achieve this? In the first place, they make their bodies commit to memory ways of behaving that will tend to reduce their exposure to violence.

But 'this fear, which served originally as a safety device, a kind of protective mechanism for the weak, finally becomes death for the self.'[11] The choice between the ghetto or suicide provokes *deception*. But the deception cultivated to enable survival corrodes the soul. Only sincerity can achieve social equality. Contact without fellowship – the pattern of segregation – leads to *hate*. 'Hatred becomes a device by which an individual seeks to protect himself against moral disintegration. He does to other human beings what he could not ordinarily do to them without losing his self-respect.'[12] Hate can generate energy and resolve, but ends up destroying everybody. 'The logic of the development of hatred is death to the spirit and disintegration of ethical and moral values.'[13]

---

11 Thurman, *Jesus and the Disinherited*, p. 35.

12 Thurman, *Jesus and the Disinherited*, p. 72.

13 Thurman, *Jesus and the Disinherited*, p. 77.

To act justly is therefore to withstand the impulse towards fear, deception and hatred. As Thurman puts it, the masses of people:

> live with their backs constantly against the wall. They are the poor, the disinherited, the dispossessed. What does our religion say to them? The issue is not what it counsels them to do for others whose need may be greater, but what religion offers to meet their own needs. The search for an answer to this question is perhaps the most important religious quest of modern life.[14]

Here is a recentring to underly all attempts to seek justice.

---

14 Thurman, *Jesus and the Disinherited*, p. 3.

PART 4

Reconceiving Justice

The argument of this book is more like a circle than a straight line. We began with a survey of what justice is and aspires to; we end with a more precise location of where justice sits and what struggles to correct injustice are truly trying to achieve. This part begins with a sober recognition of the limits of justice, even at its fairest and most earnestly sought. It then proposes that justice can only be fully understood as a manifestation of worship. And the book concludes by discovering that efforts at justice are analogies to, outworkings of, and renewal of, the notion of church. As the Epilogue affirms, far from being alternatives, rivals or opposites, justice and church are indispensable to and inseparable from one another.

10

Realize

We have seen, first, how justice is the realization and approximation in this life of the anticipated joyful co-existence with God, one another and the wider creation anticipated and promised in the next. We have noted, second, how a major project of any society is to establish institutions to advance justice and address injustice; how close attention is required to cultivate respect for and adherence to the conventions these institutions assume; and how considerable vigilance is needed to scrutinize deviations from that respect and adherence. We have recognized, third, that the definitive location from which to understand justice is that of those who have their backs to the wall; and that, in the words of Frederick Douglass, 'Power concedes nothing without a demand. It never did, and it never will'; but also, that injustice is often structural, and must be overturned not simply by identifying culprits and holding individuals to account, but by drawing whole societies to see a future beyond the imprisoning and impoverishing practices they may have taken for granted.

In this fourth and final part of the book, it is time to reconceive justice. This begins with identifying the limits of justice: to realize and appreciate what justice can't be or do. There are three parts to this. (1) Justice cannot address everything that's wrong with the world.

(2) Sometimes the pursuit of justice can jeopardize other good things. And (3), to have achieved justice, even if it were possible, is not to have attained everything to be desired in this life.

So, first, justice cannot address everything that's wrong with the world. There are many things wrong with the world that are not specifically unjust. Injustice and wrong have, at most, overlapping but not identical meanings; sometimes, almost entirely different meanings. Sweatshops in developing countries produce such goods as clothing, coffee, shoes, toys, chocolate and rugs. Such factories draw on the labour of an estimated 250 million children aged 5 to 14; of the adults who work in such conditions, 90 per cent are women. There is serious and profound wrong here, but is it correct to call it injustice? Without question such conditions would contravene laws in the developed world; but in some countries, this kind of exploitation is not illegal. The language and categories of structural injustice could characterize this as complicit: it's a life that falls short of almost any aspiration for human flourishing; but it defies the two conventional approaches to injustice – the prosecution of an offender, or the exposure and transformation of a shameful secret.

Even when justice has done its best work, it's never more than a partial achievement, leaving much that needs doing left undone. Campaigning to end sweatshops is a noble pursuit, but simply closing a sweatshop is only part of the battle. Sweatshop workers in Bangladesh may be among the lowest-paid workers in the world, but without that work they would receive no pay at all.[1]

---

1 The collapse of Rana Plaza, a network of factories above a retail complex in a district of Dhaka, Bangladesh, in 2013, with 1,134 dead and 2,500 injured, brought the gaze of the

Restructuring the Bangladeshi economy is no easy task for the Bangladeshi government, let alone a well-meaning outsider, not least because it would involve a significant degree of restructuring of the world economy. Outrage isn't always the best stimulus to sustained change in complex situations. Transforming the stranglehold clothing manufacturers, retailers and sweatshop owners have on each other is good, important and valiant work, but it doesn't fit easily into the urgent desire for the rapid and visible achievement of justice. Rescuing individuals from the grip of such hardship may be a rewarding, inspiring and attractive project, especially if the individual has talents and commitments that may make them a compelling advocate for those left behind – but removing one person and leaving the rest can hardly be described as justice: perhaps even the opposite. Thus, not every good act can fall under the heading of justice and even if justice is followed, not every good outcome is possible, at least in the short or medium term. Establishing a chain of garment factories across Bangladesh that pay decent wages and offer respectful conditions may be part of a move towards a better future; but it's a stretch to call it justice work in any conventional definition and it risks being counterproductive by putting all other local garment factories out of business.

On a different front, justice, however conscientiously pursued, can create its own casualties. When we think of casualties of justice, we most commonly consider those who have been poorly treated by the justice system

---

world on these issues. But there have been over 100 similar dangerous incidents since then. See 'The Rana Plaza accident and its aftermath', *International Labour Organisation*, www. ilo.org/global/topics/geip/WCMS_614394/lang--en/index.htm, accessed 28.1.2022.

– notably those wrongfully convicted, injured by law-enforcement officials or arrested on no proper grounds. But even when no unjust procedure has been followed or verdict reached, justice can create many casualties. While a person may decide she has nothing to gain from pursuing a legal case, she may be put under pressure by those who want to attack the party that's damaged her, whether or not they have her interests at heart. Even if they do, she can quickly be trodden down by unwelcome media attention, find her prospects for promotion at work have evaporated, or discover she will never be able to throw off being identified with a celebrated case. As is often said, there are no winners.

Or consider the situation of a child whose parent is accused of criminal activity with another child. The original child may have had only positive experiences of that parent; and yet, in being quite probably removed from the household, often finding the parents separate, invariably the offending parent incarcerated, the original child's security and well-being is dismantled – because the cause of criminal justice proceeds in a way that harms an entirely innocent bystander. In truth, few who come into contact with the criminal justice system emerge the stronger for it. It's a system that produces casualties in all directions, most painfully those too junior to have any say in proceedings; that includes not just wards of court, but children born in prison. And that's before the inequities of the system – the disproportionate number of minorities prosecuted, the inadequacy of funding given to enable those who can't afford their own counsel to defend themselves – are considered. Legal justice is a very blunt instrument for upholding the weak or defending the vulnerable. It's a very unusual victim of sexual assault who finds their case comes to court; and many who get that far come to grieve the trauma of being expected to relive the circumstances that led them there.

Perhaps the most obvious, though infrequently mentioned, flaw in the ideal of justice is that legal justice is often incapable of achieving the thing most dearly sought: restitution. A guilty verdict at a murder trial cannot deliver the one thing most yearned for: the return of the deceased loved one. Such a verdict can achieve vindication, clarity, understanding, validation, retribution, but while these are often taken to equate to justice, they are simply conventions. Justice cannot provide the thing that's most important. The trial may be finished, the guilty imprisoned, the book written, the media frenzy over; yet the gnawing grief and harrowing loss remains, and the bereaved, too often, are alone.

One approach to addressing some of this grief is justice that demands restoration: the practice of bringing the perpetrator of a crime face-to-face with the victim, or relative of the victim.[2] If you're beaten up and robbed by a teenager you recognize from your own neighbourhood, it may damage your confidence and leave you feeling violated and vulnerable. There may be a court process; the perpetrator may be punished. But you're left with abiding questions: 'Why did you do it?' 'Did you really think you'd get away with it?' 'Did you imagine I'd have anything worth stealing?' 'Was it something you had against me, or could it have been anyone who looked like an easy target?' Restorative justice is the process by which those who are willing to meet can get to the bottom of such questions, in a safe, accessible, non-judgemental context, and thus can victim or

---

2 See the Restorative Justice Council, 'What is restorative justice?', *Restorative Justice Council*, https://restorativejustice. org.uk/what-restorative-justice, accessed 29.12.2021.

perpetrator, or both, start to let go of the hold the incident has over their lives. Answers may be mundane or revealing: 'My mate put me up to it.' 'I never thought you'd tell the police.' 'It was a ritual to join a gang.' 'I was high on drugs.' 'I needed money to pay a debt.' 'I wanted to show the others I was as hard as them.' The point is, justice, in the sense of vindication and restitution, may be an illusion, and the humiliation or punishment of the offender may not take away the pain and loss, but restorative justice can address the things you didn't know you needed, and in fact turn out to be more important: your sense of understanding, your faith in human nature, your ability to make relationship, and find answers, and let go.

And so to the second part of what justice can't be or do: sometimes the pursuit of justice can jeopardize other goods. Just as the person engaged in business may use many or all relationships to advance an agenda of monetizing a product and making a profit, so the person intent on building a coalition for a just end can turn every friend, acquaintance or neighbour into part of the project of building a movement and realizing their goal. The good of justice is to enable right relationships and other kinds of flourishing by taking away major obstacles that inhibit such forms of healthy life. But sometimes the quest to remove those obstacles eradicates all potential for flourishing and right relationship once those obstacles have gone. Either the quest exhausts those involved, or the means used diminish the trust on which relationship and flourishing are based, or the whole process becomes like an addiction, making all those it envelops incapable of enjoying the fruits of success (or coping with the results of failure). Meanwhile, taking a case through the courts can harden enmity from an experience of hurt and anger into a cross-generational feud with no foreseeable end.

Early in his reign, King Solomon was asked to judge a case between two sex workers, each of whom claimed that a baby was hers. Solomon said, 'Bring me a sword ... Divide the living boy in two; then give half to one, and half to the other.' One woman protested, saying, 'Please, my lord, give her the living boy; certainly do not kill him!' The other consented, saying, 'It shall be neither mine nor yours; divide it.' Solomon said, 'Give the first woman the living boy; do not kill him. She is his mother.'[3] It's also a parable about litigation more generally. It can so easily end up 'dividing the baby' – destroying the thing both parties claim most to value. What passes as justice takes out the human factors and simply addresses commonly attested facts; but these facts, once removed from the case, make the dispute incoherent. There is much division and dispute in the world – but the cold and heavy hand of justice is not always the best way to resolve it. The true mother of the boy in the story understood that – indeed, it was an inspired way to discover which one she was.

Much of the reason for this lies with an adversarial system. An adversarial system assumes that if the rival parties are represented by well-trained advocates, and umpired by an impartial judge, the truth at the heart of the issue will surface. Experienced lawyers sometimes speak of a patient going into the operating theatre and finding, to your left, a surgeon seeking to heal you, and to your right, a surgeon working hard to kill you. Even if you emerge alive, it's unlikely you'll do so without significant damage; and some of the damage may derive

---

3 1 Kings 3.16–27.

from the things the healing surgeon has to do to you to offset the injuries incurred by the other one. The experience may remind you of the expression, 'The operation was a complete success; unfortunately, the patient died.' In terms of seeking justice, this can mean that the money expended approaches or even exceeds the settlement won; the time exhausted can never be restored; the anxiety, exasperation and strained relationships would constitute a punishment if they weren't considered part of one's investment in the case.

When two passionate opponents each assert not very good examples of fiercely held convictions, the court-room can become a uniquely poor forum for settling their disagreement. On 10 April 2019 the Australian rugby union player Israel Folau responded to a decision in Tasmania for the optional listing of gender on birth certificates by posting on Instagram, 'Warning – Drunks, Homosexuals, Adulterers, Liars, Fornicators, Thieves, Atheists, Idolaters: hell awaits you. Repent! Only Jesus saves.' A month later, an independent panel found that Folau had breached the terms of his employment by departing from Rugby Australia's commitment to inclusiveness and diversity, a commitment Folau, like all international players, had freely signed up to. Folau's contract was accordingly terminated. Folau responded by maintaining that no Australian of any faith should be fired for practising religion. Rugby Australia's supporters pointed out that Folau's remarks had crossed a line between religion and bigotry and that saying a vulnerable group (the LGBTI+ community) was going to hell en bloc encouraged others to take violent action, which constituted a hate crime. Folau's supporters said that his remarks, however inflammatory and ill-considered, could find warrant in the Bible, and therefore constituted justifiable free speech; while the Australian captain freely expressed his (contrasting) political views on social media without attracting official censure. Others brought in a wider range of reference, alleging that Rugby Australia reflected the concerns of privileged Australians, and Folau was experiencing what Islanders invariably discovered: that their convictions were of no account and thus what was being presented as a matter of gender inclusion was more broadly a case of racial exclusion.

After six months of trying to pursue the case through the courts, the parties came to a settlement in December 2019, in which Rugby Australia recognized unintentional hurt caused to Folau, and Folau acknowledged unintentional hurt to the game of rugby.[4] Both sides held passionate convictions and assumed the law existed to back those convictions. The respective parties had profoundly conflicting notions of justice, and of what freedom or inclusion actually entails. They both believed they were acting justly: but the courts proved an inadequate forum for doing so.

The third sober limit of justice is that to have achieved justice, even if it were possible, is not to have attained everything to be desired in this life. To those with only a hammer in their pocket, everything looks like a nail: it can sometimes seem that, if a legal route is available, all problems in life should be seen through a legal lens. But justice is only one of four virtues, according to Aristotle; or seven, according to Augustine; while for Thomas

---

4 Mike Hytner, 'Israel Folau and Rugby Australia settle unfair dismissal claim over social media post', *The Guardian*, 4 December 2019, https://www.theguardian.com/sport/2019/dec/04/israel-folau-and-rugby-australia-settle-unfair-dismissal-claim-over-social-media-post, accessed 30.12.2021.

Aquinas, love is the form of all seven, including justice, and all the other six are expressions of love. In other words, justice may be a place to begin, but it is almost never a place to end; and to achieve justice requires not only just laws and just procedures, but just people. If you have just people, you may have most of what you were looking for justice to provide. There is, in the end, no highest court of human affairs and no guarantee that those affairs will always fall on the side of justice; there is no security that the arc of history tends towards justice, despite the nobility and integrity of many who have suggested so; there is only the slow and laboured establishment of convention and the gradual marshalling of public opinion around principles that uphold the weak and defend the vulnerable, and those who passionately seek justice often find themselves ahead of that slow arc and in defiance of public consensus.

And even when victory is achieved, and right prevails, and the battle seems over, the real work is still to begin: because the real work is not to compel all people to share one's convictions and embody one's standards, but to find ways to live in peace with those who, whether by sincere sentiment or lax commitment, don't. Otherwise, the phrase 'There can be no peace without justice' is simply replaced by a contrasting fact: that the declaration of justice is the start of a new war.

11

Become

The previous chapters have described several understandings of justice. Those who seek good judgement
spend a lot of time trying to make the law work for
them. Those who seek good order are busy trying to
make society function. Those who seek redistributive
justice are struggling to set right what justice and order
have left unfinished. All three groups dispute each other's
notion of justice; and all three groups, as the previous
chapter has shown, are often disappointed when they
find what their own notion is incapable of achieving.

How then to begin to act justly? In his survey com-
paring the best human efforts at justice with the divine
vision, Augustine makes an intriguing yet telling assertion. Augustine accepts the understanding Cicero puts
in the mouth of Scipio in the former's book, *On the
Republic*: a commonwealth is 'an assembly united in
fellowship by common agreement as to what is right and
a community of interests'. Scipio also describes a society
as a 'partnership in justice'.[1] Then Augustine argues that
'where there is no true justice there can be no right.' But
here he introduces a customary notion of justice: 'Justice

---

[1] Both references are made in Augustine, *The City of God*,
2:21, and are repeated at 19:21. The rest of the discussion in this
paragraph all concerns 19:21.

is that virtue which gives everyone [their] due.' Which
enables him to make the decisive move: to maintain that
if humans cannot say to God, 'I am giving you your due'
– which indeed they cannot, when they are worshipping
other gods or none at all – then they cannot claim to be
giving each their due, and therefore cannot claim to be
upholding justice. Thus, since God was not worshipped
in ancient Rome, justice never prevailed there, and the
Roman Empire was not truly a society. Indeed, says
Augustine, there never has been a just society – there
never has been a true partnership in justice; there have
only been societies united by 'common objects of love'
– generally, the desire for peace. Augustine's claim therefore is that without true worship, there can be no justice.

This claim has sometimes been treated in a highly
assertive way, as if to say only a Christian society can
be a truly just society – a claim for which the historical
evidence is poor. But it does not need to be taken this
way. It can be taken in a much humbler vein. It simply
means to recognize that justice is the establishment of
good conventions around 'common objects of love' and
that to set up good conventions needs not only reflection
on experience, but a hierarchy of goods. A hierarchy of
goods requires an honest appraisal of relative values –
or appreciation of different degrees of worth. Another
name for the apportionment of differing levels of worth
and valorizing of the highest level is worship. Hence,
right worship is the beginning of true justice. In other
words, what Christians are doing by worshipping God
is indeed praising God for God's own sake – but in addition, worshipping God is so ordering their loves and
their lives as to elicit justice.

At the centre of Christian worship is the Bible. An
understanding of justice as apportioning appropriate

levels of worth suggests a renewed way of thinking about the Bible. It means perceiving the Bible as a book about justice. When the Pharisees are told, 'You shall love the Lord your God with all your heart, and with all your soul, and with all your mind' and 'You shall love your neighbour as yourself', they are being given the principles of worship and ethics – or justice, where worship and ethics meet.[2] In many ways, you can read the Old Testament as a story about what happens to justice when worship goes astray.

There are 100 references to justice in the Scriptures. Almost all are to be found in the Old Testament. The most concentrated treatment of justice comes in Isaiah 42. Here God announces that justice is to be done by a servant. These are the words of love spoken by God to this servant: 'I uphold you. You are my chosen one. You delight my soul. I have put my spirit upon you.' It turns out that this servant is a person of action rather than words: no loud cries or shouting in the street. And this servant has a compassionate heart: if you are broken or fragile (a 'bruised reed' or a 'dimly burning wick'), this servant will look out for you. This servant won't be subdued by enemies, or the greatness of the task, and won't pause until the whole task is finished, right out to the edges of the land. It's a vast and grand agenda.

Why is God sending this servant? To fulfil the purpose for which Israel was originally called. In Genesis 12, God called Abraham and his descendants to be the ones through whom all peoples found a blessing. That's precisely what this servant is being sent to be. What does that blessing look like? Verse 7 says, 'To open the eyes that are blind, to bring out the prisoners from

---

2 Matthew 22.37–40.

the dungeon'. It's not a comment about disability and political prisoners. It's a statement about exile. Isaiah 42 is the first of four so-called Servant Songs in the middle chapters of Isaiah that are saying to Israel, 'You're at your lowest ebb, you've lost land, king and temple – but I am choosing you to be at the centre of my purposes for all creation. You've lost sight of me, but I'm going to open your eyes. You're languishing in exile, but I'm going to bring you home.' 'The former things have come to pass' – in other words, I brought you out of slavery in Egypt. 'The new things I now declare' – in other words, I'm about to bring you back from Babylon.

Isaiah identifies two crucial dimensions of justice. The first is right relationship. Just as you can't run an organization by an organizational chart – because an organization isn't a machine, it's an organism, made up of relationships – so justice is the same. When two parties walk away from a law court, as we have seen, at least one of them is generally bitter and thwarted. Winning and losing isn't the best way to ensure respect, dignity, honour and grace, which is what a healthy set of relationships looks like. Isaiah's concerns are right relationships with God and one another; today we'd add the planet. This is what justice is about.

But in the end, justice, for Isaiah, is about a person. A person who embodies right relationship. God's servant. In the story of Jesus' baptism, God says, 'This is my Son, the Beloved, with whom I am well pleased.'[3] These words reinterpret Isaiah 42.1: 'Here is my servant, whom I uphold, my chosen, in whom my soul delights; I have put my spirit upon him.' What Matthew is saying is that Jesus is the servant of Isaiah 42. This explains why

---

3 Matthew 3.13–17.

Jesus proceeds to open people's eyes and set them free of their bondage to sin, illness, debt and exclusion. He enacts justice – or, in Isaiah's words, 'He brings forth justice to the nations.' Justice is, in the end, a person who models and embodies right relationship with God and one another.

Thus, Christians have a word for justice: that word is Jesus. If justice is giving each their due, then the hierarchy of estimation begins with recognizing what is due to the God of Jesus Christ. Worship is in truth worthship; thus, it's worship that ultimately sets the scales of justice. Here's what God says to those who come to be baptized: 'I uphold you. You are my chosen one. You delight my soul. I have put my spirit upon you.' That's the first part. This is the second part: 'You will not grow faint or be crushed until you have established justice in the earth.' And this is the last part: 'Today I send my Holy Spirit upon you. I will be your shield and defender, from this time forward and for evermore.' Baptism is the moment God's children become servants of justice.

The task therefore is to understand how worship is a setting-forth of Jesus and an embodiment of God's kingdom that anticipates heaven and depicts justice. This can only happen if justice and worship are understood to be in a reciprocal relationship by which each refines the understanding of the other.

Public worship is the definitive way the life of the church is ordered so as to imitate and anticipate the life of heaven. Heaven is fully to be with God, oneself, one another and the renewed creation. So worship aspires to embody that expectation. We may here consider two kinds of worship stipulated by Jesus: the Eucharist, about which he said, 'Do this in remembrance of me'; and footwashing, about which he said, 'If I, your Lord and Teacher, have washed your feet, you also ought to wash one another's feet.'[4]

The Eucharist is, as an elemental social process, an event in which an assembly of God's people bring to the table their differences – their different wealth, expressed in the money offering, their diverse gifts, expressed in the bread and the wine, their different sins, articulated in the confession, their adversarial differences with one another, addressed in the sharing of the peace – and receive back the same: the body and blood of Christ. God's people bring their scarcity – their folly, fear, faithlessness, falsehood, fragility – and receive back God's abundance: forgiveness and eternal life. God's people bring forward their mortality – their inability to change their heritage or alter their destiny – and receive back God's divinity: a healed past and a limitless future. The Eucharist is therefore an embodiment of the justice of God, which paradoxically is not justice, as conventionally understood, but mercy: 'There is no one who does good, no, not one.' 'If you, O LORD, should mark iniquities, Lord, who could stand?'[5]

But every part of this process must be mutually enriched and refined by the practice of justice. Thus, everyone is equal around the table, everyone may be incorporated into Christ's body in baptism. But is everyone represented in the language of the hymns? Is everyone visible in representative roles? Is everyone's tradition audible in styles of music? Are everyone's dietary needs catered for in the distributed elements? Is everyone's diversity included in the way words and gestures are shared? Is everyone's gender identity blessed

---

4 Luke 22.19; John 13.14.
5 Psalm 14.3; 130.3.

in the words of benediction? Is everyone's calling honoured in the way God's people are sent out to love and serve? Do monuments in the building commemorate those whose wealth was created through the exploitation of others? Does the wood of the seats come from a sustainable forest? Does the paper or the service order or the electricity used to project information fit into a community pattern of carbon-neutral commitment? Does the worship genuinely include those joining remotely? Do people's means of transport honour the planet? Is the congregation in a healthy, mutually upholding relationship with neighbours near and far across social and economic divides? Is it putting its energies to use to foster justice and respond to injustice? And is the community maximizing the gifts it's been given by bringing its diverse people into genuine and ennobling relationship with one another, by finding ways for the old to be taught by the young and the young entertained by the old, by walking with one another the path of forgiveness, by facing together the hardest truths of grief and death and separation and hurt, by forming a supportive circle around the addicted or the shamed or the incarcerated, by taking steps into prayer with the asylum seeker or journeys into solitude with those who are neurodiverse?

This process must be genuinely two-way. We can't start to imagine there's a thing called 'justice' that sits in one-directional judgement over something always pedestrian called worship. So is the liturgy being allowed to shed light on those things in life often taken for granted? When clergy and perhaps choir walk in procession behind a cross, is this practice given scope to critique other emblems we follow or marches we tread? When a congregation stands to sing 'Glory to God in the highest heaven', is this practice permitted to shed light on other kinds of glory and others who receive adulation and acclaim? When believers stand and place a hand on their heart to profess their faith in the words of the creed, is this practice allowed to cast into question any other pledge of allegiance? When the faithful kneel to intercede, does this have any bearing on whence true blessings are perceived to come? The similarities between a worship service and a rock concert, a sports game, a legislative chamber, a military parade ground or a courtroom are neither coincidental nor superficial: these are the places we act out our highest commitments and aspirations.

The significance of footwashing is that it is a lowly, humiliating task – since feet in the New Testament are locations of soil and filth, and sometimes a cipher for genital intimacy – yet it becomes a divinely commanded way of continually rediscovering our dependence on one another and our inability to justify any permanent status hierarchy. There was a white South African judge in Bloemfontein named Jan Christiaan Olivier. Amid controversy, after Black worshippers had been refused entry to the funeral of a white superintendent, a Black pastor invited Olivier to his church on Maundy Thursday to defuse the tension. It was a footwashing service. The pastor wanted the people to see that their love was not rejected. So he asked Olivier to wash the feet of Martha Fortuin. Thirty years earlier, Martha had gone to work in Olivier's home. She had followed him and his wife to Cape Town and Pretoria when Olivier became a judge and had returned with him to Bloemfontein when he became a justice of the court. Olivier took her foot in his hand.

And as he was doing this, he thought how far those feet had walked for his family. And suddenly he saw Martha and his own daughter when she was a child and he remembered clearly how Martha would kiss her feet. So he thought to himself, if she can kiss my daughter's feet, why can I not kiss her feet? Then he took both her feet in his hands with gentleness for they were both no doubt tired with much serving, and he kissed them both.[6]

Paul Duke notes the significance of this story. He comments that Olivier lost his political career – but perhaps found his soul. Then Duke adds:

Like him, most of us enter the room of this text thinking to be good disciples, but still wearing the title of judge, long accustomed to peering down from the high bench and pronouncing innocence or guilt, pardon or punishment on others and on ourselves, often with righteous intent. But here in this table room with Christ, we are disrobed and disarmed. We are not judged at all, but held and bathed in love. Our anxieties protest, but the Host lays a finger to our lips. Then we are brought near to sisters and brothers, all cleansed by the same grace. In them we see the love that has served us, and we move to embrace them. We emerge from such an encounter happily finished with our judicial career.[7]

Thus does footwashing redefine worship; and thus does worship realign justice.

---

6 Alan Paton, *Ah, But Your Land is Beautiful* (New York: Vintage, 2002), p. 235.

7 Paul Duke, 'John 13:1–17, 31b–35', *Interpretation: A Journal of Bible and Theology* 49/4 (1995), pp. 398–402.

12

Share

So far, I've outlined the necessity, nature, processes, struggles and limitations of justice. I've tried to map out why we should seek to act justly, and what it might mean to do so, without doing more harm than good. It's a daunting challenge, because the issues are complex, the energy and passion required are never-ending, the prospect of facing hostility is real and sometimes the likelihood of genuine success is small. Which is why it's unwise to do it alone.

It's also unnecessary. Justice is a virtue. Like all virtues, it's fostered and practised in community. This is the final part of reconceiving justice. To pursue justice is to act in solidarity with the oppressed, in collaboration with those seeking to build just institutions, and to grow in understanding of human, created and divine worth. The way to change the world isn't simply to become just. It's to join a just community; one seeking to embody and advance justice. The words of the anthropologist Margaret Mead are well known: 'Never doubt that a small group of thoughtful, committed citizens can change the world; indeed, it's the only thing that ever has.'[1] But not everyone hears those words and then joins

---

1 The quotation appears in Donald Keys, *Earth at Omega: Passage to Planetization* (Boston, MA: Branden Press, 1982), p. 79.

such a community. Christians have a word for a community of justice: they call it church.

Church is therefore the focus of the Christian pursuit of justice because church is where Christians seek right relationship with God, themselves, one another, the stranger and the whole creation. Like every quest, the journey is an education in the nature of the destination. Seeking justice refines the Christian notion of church, and church defines the Christian notion of justice. In the previous chapter, we noted a phrase that makes an appropriate designation for church: partnership in justice. This phrase discloses the intent of this whole book: that each chapter in turn contribute to a conception of church. In this final chapter I bring out the ways each foregoing chapter has defined and refined what Christians mean by church.

Thus Chapter 1, Imagine, asserts that justice begins in the imagination, which is where church also begins. Justice imagines a realm where each person flourishes, putting talents to work, finding healthy recreation, creating new life and living at peace with one another and the creation; justice then puts in place the safeguards, procedures and practices needed to 'keep the ball in play' – to enable each to have access, opportunity and belonging to live to the full, and for society as a whole to thrive by drawing out the gifts of all its members, individually and collectively. Church both receives this portrayal of a healthy society and refines it by highlighting how the equal worth of each human being is not inherent, but bestowed on humanity, humanity being the form Jesus took when embodying God's desire to be with creation: in other words, human dignity is not a birthright, but derives from being made in the image of the God seen in Christ. Likewise, the true flourishing of creation, and humanity within it, is not an impossible ideal to be nobly aspired to, but the everlasting reality of heaven that will one day be known and that all earthly strivings humbly anticipate. Church is the sphere of life where these convictions are invited to shape all other practices of life and rules of community.

Chapter 2, See, is about seeing; and seeing is an activity of the moral imagination. We act in the world that we see. The philosopher Bertrand Russell noted that, 'People seem good while they are oppressed, but they only wish to become oppressors in their turn: life is nothing but a competition to be the criminal rather than the victim.'[2] Russell's seeing reduced his view of humanity to a bare scramble for advantage: true seeing perceives beyond this scramble to all the texture of existence obscured by his words 'nothing but'. Whether seeing with the eyes of solidarity or compassion; whether hearing a story that sounds familiar but keeping on listening for the unique particulars that make it poignant, or listening to a strange diversity of sounds until a pattern and purpose emerges; whether keeping an open mind for multiple interpretations, or having a conscience trained to discern signs of sinister or underhand activity; in every case, justice requires close attention, so as neither to miss those things hidden in plain sight, nor to put two and two together and make more than four. Church sees. Church sees what is, and what could yet be. Church sees not just what a person is now, but what the Holy Spirit is making of them in God's good time. Because it has been trained to see the horror of the cross, church doesn't

2 Letter from Bertrand Russell to Ottoline Morrell, *The Selected Letters of Bertrand Russell, Volume 2: Public Years 1914–1970* (London and New York: Routledge, 2002), p. 214.

look away from evil, even – especially – among its own ranks, as if closing its eyes would make evil go away, or as if propagating falsehood were ever the way to proclaim justice and advance peace. Church trains people to see through cross to resurrection, through death to life, through pain to glory. It trusts that resurrection, life and glory are the consolations needed to stay with the horror of injustice and call it by its name – since you can only name the worst if you are confident the worst is not for ever.

The passionate quest for justice needs to be tempered and cleansed by what in Chapter 3, Recognize, I described as the recognition of one's own complicity. This is a hard truth, both because such a recognition seems to dismantle much of the energy generated by righteous indignation, and because so much of the struggle for justice (particularly when taken on by the headstrong to right others' woes) is consciously or unconsciously about assuaging guilt. But church is unsentimental about this. 'Let anyone among you who is without sin be the first to throw a stone', said Jesus to the scribes and the Pharisees. 'When you are offering your gift at the altar, if you remember that your brother or sister has something against you, leave your gift there before the altar and go; first be reconciled to your brother or sister, and then come and offer your gift', said Jesus to those overcome by anger. 'First take the log out of your own eye, and then you will see clearly to take the speck out of your neighbour's eye', says Jesus to those quick to judge.[3] Justice refines church at this point; for church has become known as a coven for hypocrites, which justice has sought to expose and cleanse. It takes humility for church – which should

---

3 John 8.7; Matthew 5.23–24; 7.5.

be the first to understand humility, since the rock on which it was founded denied Jesus moments after promising to be with him to the end – to have its hypocrisy uncovered and take lessons in humility from those who practise humility better than it does. Just as one of the great tasks of justice is to enquire who investigates the police and who tries the judiciary, so one of the great questions of church is whether it can recognize that the Holy Spirit also works through those secular agencies that hold it most fiercely to account.

A different kind of humility is in question in Chapter 4, Build: this is about having the humility to accept that the institutional structure inherited from previous generations represents their best efforts to create and sustain a pattern of life that preserved the good, averted the bad, made room for the Spirit and allowed for human nature. The passionate and the earnest will always tend to assume that the history of the church has been a litany of departures from the pristine truth available to the early disciples; but the Gospels and Acts repeatedly show how foolish were the disciples and how quarrelsome were the first leaders of the church – and how disputatious was that supposedly pristine era. The second part of this book, Constructing Justice, beginning with this fourth chapter, describes the foundations of a system of justice that can be upheld over many centuries, embodying the wisdom of past generations with the refinement of new circumstances or discovered flaws. The justice system and the church can both seem inflexible, self-absorbed, self-important and over-embellished – in many cases absurdly so – but at other times the formal apparatus helps to ensure the intensity of the moment does not dispel the wisdom of the ages. Justice reminds church of the unavoidability of judgement and the inevitability of punishment; church reminds justice of the overarching context of mercy and the ultimate goal of restoration to community.

In Chapter 5, Practise, we saw how the rule of law is like the veins and arteries of the justice system: nothing can function without it. The rule of law functions in justice in a somewhat similar way to the role of Scripture in church: it does not do all the work for you, but take it away and you have no identity, no guiding principle, no touchstone to return to. Just as in Chapter 5 we saw the crucial role for civil society in living, upholding, employing and enriching the rule of law, so in church we see the role of local congregations embodying everything Scripture proclaims. Just as we saw how talking points around sporting incidents provide a public way to explore and reassert the rule of law, so in a local congregation do the regular round of questions concerning what to do about the homeless couple who've slept the last two nights in the porch, and whether it matters that this year's accounts are late, become the touchstone moments as a community discovers where its principles lie. Justice and church remind each other that gospel can become its own law – and law can, in some cases, become gospel.

The area of scrutiny discussed in Chapter 6, Scrutinize, is a huge challenge to a church whose motivation tends to come from following a first-century figure who had no place to lay his head, left no written documents and gave no indication of his views about the tidiness of filing systems or the best way to ensure expense claims are genuine. Yet the example of a Rob Bilott sitting amid mountains of DuPont documents is not an instruction to church to obsess about detail. Instead, it's a reminder to church that faithfulness is not so much about the grand gestures as the small fidelities. In the words of the prayer of Francis Drake, 'When thou givest to thy servants to endeavour any great matter, grant us also to know that it is not the beginning, but the continuing of the same unto the end, until it be thoroughly finished, which yieldeth the true glory.'[4] Does the monk, alone in his cell, read to the very end of the psalms appointed for that night? Does the church cleaner dust on the window-sill above the height of any worshipper? Does the youth group leader check every last item on the risk register for an expedition, even if she's seen so many of these before? George Herbert claimed the words 'for thy sake' were the elixir that turned all faithful activity to gold.[5] In justice, as in church, detail is a form of love.

Chapter 7, Struggle, considers the structural nature of most injustice, and the complexity of what it means to struggle for justice when it's not as simple as oppos-ing a single egregious opponent. It's an education in how the energy and conviction of a quest turns into the more sophisticated and subtle tactics of a long-term programme. If the issue can be crystallized into a single piece of legislation or legal battle, victory may be won, but that victory may exclude many or most of the true issues underlying the struggle. Here, justice is a teacher to the church. Sometimes the daily realities of seeking holiness amid the humdrum, intractable, adversarial and

---

4 Patrick Comerford, 'Praying in the words of Sir Francis Drake', *Patrick Comerford*, 13 November 2009, http://www. patrickcomerford.com/2009/11/praying-in-words-of-sir-francis-drake.html, accessed 31.12.2021.

5 'Nothing can be so mean, Which with his tincture (for thy sake) Will not grow bright and clean ... This is the famous stone That turneth all to gold...', George Herbert, 'The Elixir', avail-able from https://www.georgeherbert.org.uk/archives/selected_work_20.html, accessed 21.3.2022.

infuriating challenges of life seem just too daunting, too unglamorous, too mundane. Sometimes those who pride themselves on being part of the solution feel like they've become part of the problem. Much as stories tend to highlight the lone hero, the lone hero can be insufferable to be around and, even if a star at overcoming evil, so full of flaws as to be a poor representative of what good might look like. Both justice and church are, at heart, a team game. This isn't about one person getting it right, despite being surrounded by imbeciles (or sinners). This is about a community of hope striving together to face obstacles and encounter them as part of an education in patience and ingenuity. The most powerful word in such a struggle is not 'victory' but 'together'.

Organizing is a challenge to church in important ways, as Chapter 8, Organize, notes – but church is also an important counter to organizing. Some years ago, before the days of mobile phones and the internet, I realized the capacity of church for organizing when a group was needed that afternoon to picket a local accountancy firm that was facilitating the takeover (perceived locally as a synonym for demise) of the local shipyard. I quickly realized I could create a pyramid of phone calls cascading throughout the congregation and its contacts – and sure enough, that afternoon, 15 people appeared with me on the accountancy firm's doorstep. There were only two other protestors from outside the church network. The church's power to organize outdid any other local pressure group by a considerable margin. That taught me that church is about organizing – not just in the face of economic hardship, but in every aspect of life. For the triumph of good, what is needed is to be better organized than evil. This is where much of the real work of church lies. Organizing has a great deal to teach church, especially in seeing the abundance of what it has been given, and not merely the scarcity: in this way, justice is often more faithful to the gospel than church is. Organizing has an important role in teaching the church how to approach conflict, and when to see tension as a creative force for bringing difference to a head and holding the powerful to account. But church has some things to refine organizing: notably the latter's tendency to instrumentalize relationships for achieving goals, which can impoverish all participants, not just those called to keep their promises.

Chapter 9, Support, contains important lessons for those who see 'church' as the centre of a project called 'world'. Justice can easily become a campaign to place oneself at the centre of all things – a project of self-justification drawn from a desire to think well of oneself; and one common way to think well of oneself is to create strategies by which one can imagine oneself better than other people. This pattern has been the curse of church since the beginning. To witness in this chapter the potential pitfalls of international aid and allyship is to perceive secular manifestations of a perennial church problem. 'Outdo one another in showing honour', says Paul; but that can easily turn into a competition where I win because I see how poorly you perform.[6] Howard Thurman's challenge is for church to see Jesus' social context as normative. This is humbling for many activists for justice, for it can be tempting to assume justice is something the comfortable take up as a project to prove their virtue before resuming their normal and appropriate condition of being comfortable. Thurman argues that those whose social circumstances resemble those of

---

6 Romans 12.10.

Jesus' people in first-century Palestine best understand and define what the questions of justice – and of church – truly are. This isn't just a matter for those seeking to work for justice – it's a transformative challenge for anyone invested in church.

The phrase, 'Vengeance is mine, I will repay, says the Lord',[7] is among the most misunderstood in Scripture; but it's the key to comprehending the significance of Chapter 10, Realize. Seeking justice is not always the route to fulfilment, satisfaction or peace, since there are things that justice, even once technically achieved, can never bring – and sometimes justice can come, but those other blessings are further away than before. Here, church can refine justice. 'Vengeance is mine' does not mean God delights in vindictive punishment. It means that sometimes we cannot find our way to justice, and we have to leave the conclusion of a story to God, and trust that it's with God that accountability for the wrongdoer and vindication for the victim best lies. Meanwhile, it's on those other blessings – peace, reconciliation, forgiveness, joy, love – that church properly focuses. For church, justice is a route to those things, not an end in itself: it's usually an indispensable route, but it's never more than part of the journey; and sometimes it proves to be a detour.

Finally, and most obviously, worship is the heart of church. Chapter 11, Become, demonstrates why and how this is so. But what the discussion in Augustine's *City of God* makes clear is that worship is the heart of justice also. Church is fundamentally about cherishing God – giving God God's due. Meanwhile, justice is giving human beings – and now we would say the planet

---

7 Deuteronomy 32.35, quoted in Romans 12.19.

and the whole creation also – their due. Thomas Aquinas speaks of the virtue of religion. Religion, he says, is a part of what it means to be just, because religion gives God God's due as the source of all being and the giver of all good things.[8] Justice refines church by highlighting ways in which we honour God by honouring one another and by showing how we learn better to honour God by learning better how to honour one another. In a children's story, Monkey and Elephant decide to be friends.[9] Monkey knows everything about friendship, but Elephant confesses to being a beginner. Monkey sets the agenda and proceeds with little regard for Elephant, exploiting and ignoring his purported friend. At each turn, Elephant says, ingenuously from him, but increasingly ironically to the reader, 'Is that what friends do?' Eventually, Monkey has to face some hard truths. It's a children's story; but it's not just a children's story. It's an analogy of the relationship between justice and church. Each says to the other, 'Is that what justice means? Is that what just people do?' And each finds itself sometimes the teacher, sometimes the pupil. As they will continue to be, until justice and peace embrace.[10]

---

8 Thomas Aquinas, *Summa Theologiae* II–II, p. 81. Religion is not a theological virtue for Aquinas, because its immediate object is not God, but rather the reverence due to God: it is the first among the moral virtues. The virtue of religion is enacted through adoration, prayer, sacrifice, oblation and vows. Opposition to religion is enacted through neglect of prayer, blasphemy, tempting God, sacrilege, perjury, simony, idolatry and superstition. Atheism is considered a sin against religion.

9 Marjorie Newman, illustrated by Peter Bowman, *Is That What Friends Do?* (London: Hutchinson, 1998).

10 Psalm 85.10 reads, 'Steadfast love and faithfulness will meet: righteousness and peace will kiss each other.' I haven't referred to Nicholas Wolterstorff in this book, because his

For, in the end, justice is not something I have in my mind that I perceive you don't have, and then I work beside you, cajoling, policing, persuading, demanding, forcing or prosecuting you until you embody justice as admirably as I do. Justice is something out of reach of us both, and something I try to exemplify in my institution, organization or association, in my choices, in my community, in my use of resources, in my way of forming sustainable life, in my relating to the stranger, in my mercy towards those who've hurt me, in my humility before those I've harmed, in my confronting of the criminal, the horrendous and the wrong – and which you, too, assume, rely on, invest in and promote in your no doubt different way from mine. I strive to act justly because I seek to inhabit the world that I believe God is bringing into being and will one day fully usher in – and I wish to be trained to belong in that world and learn to take its habits for granted. That's what being a Christian means. Part of that training is to understand that there are ways the church profoundly fails, and there are ways the Holy Spirit works more obviously and more actively in the world beyond the church. I'm still discovering, I'm still failing, I'm still in need of the wisdom and guidance

---

extensive treatment of justice in Scripture is something I simply assume, and his foundational place for rights has a different emphasis from mine. But I am nonetheless indebted to his three books, *Until Justice and Peace Embrace: The Kuyper Lectures for 1981 Delivered at the Free University of Amsterdam* (Grand Rapids, MI: Eerdmans, 1983), *Justice: Rights and Wrongs* (Princeton, NJ: Princeton University Press, 2010) and *Journey Toward Justice: Personal Encounters in the Global South* (Grand Rapids, MI: Eerdmans, 2013), the last of which was formative for my thinking when I wrote *A Nazareth Manifesto: Being With God* (Oxford: Wiley-Blackwell, 2015).

of others to light my path. That's not a reason to give up on myself or to give up on justice; it's a reason to look from side to side, be grateful for those walking beside me, church or otherwise, be glad for being given good work to do; and begin again.

Epilogue: Climate Justice

The facts of the climate emergency are widely known. The rise in global temperatures, accelerating at an alarming rate, is already having profound effects around the world in acute weather events, vulnerability of food supplies and rising sea levels. We now face the prospect of a sequence of progressively extreme consequences. These begin with increasing prevalence of intense and violent conflicts as access to energy and safe places to live is made more difficult. They move on to parts of the world becoming uninhabitable, species being decimated and rates of migration increasing beyond our current imagination. They eventually reach human life becoming unsustainable because of severe weather, the depletion of resources, or conflict over those resources becoming universal, permanent and brutal.

I'm not going to dwell on the severity, speed and extent of the climate crisis because everyone knows we have a very serious problem. Those who deny it aren't going to be moved by evidence or graphic detail. Those who get it in their head but haven't translated that into their heart or their hand aren't going to be motivated by overwhelming and depressing data. What we each need is a sense of what we can actually do. So I want to set out a series of five concentric circles, like ripples in a pond in which you've just dropped a pebble. Think of a person living in two generations' time, potentially facing the extreme consequences I've outlined, and imagine what they'd be saying to you about what they wish you'd done differently. I'm going to set out what I suppose they might say, in five concentric circles, starting in the middle, with the simplest.

We begin with humility. It's the beginning of the gospel: repent. Recognize how up to your neck your life is in the practices and habits that have got us into this mess. Don't begin by hectoring the fuel extractors or denouncing the grossest emitters or berating the ozone destroyers. Accept that almost all of us are immersed in a system that has made ecological depletion the inevitable fallout from human mastery of the planet. See it this way: there's humanity, the centre of the story; there's everything else that grows on or lives in or inhabits the planet; and there's limitation – be it limited length of life, or strength, or speed of movement, or comfort, or breadth of diet, or a hundred other things. For centuries now we've been playing a game, which goes like this: how can humanity use those other constituent elements of this planet in its fundamental project of overcoming its limitations? Everything – be it silicon, titanium, oil or ivory – has been corralled into this project. Almost every strategy for addressing climate change has been about working out how we can find renewable resources with which to continue this project. When will the time come when we start to question the very foundations of the project itself – the idea that we spend our time on earth seeking to overcome limitation by using those living or inanimate things with which we share our ecosystem?

When I say repent, I don't simply mean 'Continue to consume at exponentially increasing rates, but be sure to check those resources are renewable.' I mean spend serious time reflecting on how much of our lives is shaped by the assumption that our mission is to make life that little bit longer, run the race that bit faster, eat food that bit more exotic, wear clothes that bit more stylish. Somebody has to pay for all these things we call progress, and further down the food chain, beyond low-wage workers and unsavoury animal conditions, comes the finitude of the earth and eventually life itself, of which this whole project is a denial. Humility means facing the truth that we're all invested up to our necks in this project. So we're not calling on some nefarious Them to change their behaviour, or a parental government to fix things for us. We're realizing that if I want the world to change, I need to let that change begin with me. And it's not about being forced to change – it's about genuinely wanting to. That's the first circle: humility.

The second circle is solidarity. Lying at the root of so many of the great leaps of progress was a sense of escape – that those in possession of the new technology could not only escape from the limitations of being human, but could get beyond and out of reach of the great mass of humankind into a place of safety, comfort and fulfil-ment. Likewise, at the root of much of the denial and complacency of the last 40 years has been the sense that it won't actually affect me. It may be tough on Venice, Bangladesh and the Maldives, but I'll have access to enough protective devices to seal me off from whatever damage it does. This is one reason why the pandemic clarifies some of the issues about the ecological crisis. Coronavirus is not something you can easily seal your-self off from. It's no respecter of wealth or status. Like the climate emergency, those with resources can more often find a degree of amelioration. But the rich and fit and young die too, or are bereaved, or experience debilitating long-term effects.

Solidarity changes our notion of the word 'we'. The pandemic has exposed the absurdity of thinking any of us, individually, locally or nationally, can seal ourselves away. The climate emergency is the same. Even if you're not living on a sea-level island or farming temperature-sensitive crops, the effects will reach you soon enough. There's only one 'we' now – and that's the global 'we'. The only way to address the pandemic is as a global community. What used to be charity or imperial paternalism is now simply enlightened self-interest. It's like the difference between the ethics of wearing a seat belt and of smoking a cigarette. Not wearing a seat belt endangers yourself. Smoking a cigarette endangers everyone around you. There's no individual climate crisis. It's an everybody thing. But the 'we' in the climate emergency isn't just about everyone today. It's about everyone who comes after us. 'We' now includes all future life on this planet, for hundreds, thousands, millions of years. It's a big 'we'. There's no escaping it. The climate emergency is spoken of as a question of survival; but before it's about survival, it's about justice.

The third circle, building on humility and solidarity, is example. What inspires? Example. What changes hearts and minds? Example. What empowers the inhibited, dismantles inertia, outflanks cynicism? Example. Let me take you by the hand and walk you, online or tangibly, round the initiatives, communities and projects around the world, and show you something that will make you change your mind. It's all in the word 'show'. We can protest, we can march, we can boycott, we can vilify, we can picket, we can sabotage, we can research, we can lobby, we can campaign; but what really changes the imagination is example. It's in the imagination that transformation really happens. A church is not fundamentally a building: it's a living example of what the Holy Spirit can do among people committed to pool their assets, work together, seek a beautiful life and open the windows to let God in. A church is built on those two concentric circles – humility, because none of us can do this alone, and solidarity, because together we can be more than the sum of our parts, we can be one body whose many members all have a vital role to play.

Let's imagine I was to ask everyone in my own church, 'What do you belong to?' Many would say St Martin's. Some would say a political party, or a national institution, or a trade or professional body. Some would have looser affiliations, like a daily newspaper they subscribe to or a neighbourhood association they support. Let's estimate how many we'd each have. There's likely a lot of overlap, so we'll call it five. And at an average worship service there are maybe 200 people in the building and 150 online. That's 15,000 affiliations between us. Imagine we said, 'I'm going to make it my business to use all my influence to make each of those organizations an ecological example.' An example of humility and solidarity – about fuel, about food, about waste, about air quality, about local sourcing of products, about all the things we all need to take for granted. This is how a society changes, not simply by government directives – we've all seen the complexity and inequity of that during the pandemic – but by changing what we all take for granted, what people disapprove of but tolerate and what people no longer tolerate. It's happening about race, about gender equality, about sexuality, about online hatred. It needs to happen about ecology. It's what church is about. You try to set an example – you fail – people point the finger – but what do you do then? You don't stop trying. You try harder. That's the transformation of example.

We've considered humility, solidarity and example. The fourth concentric circle is accountability. Accountability names the way in which people who generally think of themselves as powerless, or small cogs in a big machine, get to bring about large-scale change. When we're talking about governments, or multinational corporations, a lot of us can feel there's little we can do. In fact, what we can do comes down to three questions. We ask, 'What state do you want the world to be in in 50 years' time?' Then we ask, 'What are you going to do about it?' Then we ask, 'And have you done it?' When we look to influential conferences, we consider the first two questions. But when we look at the climate crisis as a whole, we mustn't lose sight of the third question. We're simply saying, 'Keep your promises.' We want to extract more far-reaching promises. But promises count for little if they're not kept. Accountability is the name for the way we hold people to the promises they've made. All the climate conferences in the world will be in vain if we celebrate promises made that are not kept.

The irony of the climate crisis is that, because of the prominence of Extinction Rebellion and other such campaigns, climate change has been associated with protest movements concerned with struggle and organizing. That's not where it should belong. It should be about the justice system and the rule of law. The climate emergency has exposed the absence of and the need for international structures of the kind Western nations worked so hard to create for themselves decades or centuries ago.

You may say that there's nothing especially Christian about the first four circles. That's back to humility.

Christians have to accept that their notion of heaven has too often been used as a form of escape that protected them while others were lost, and that their notion of salvation has too often been seen as a kind of technology that enabled their mastery over human limitation. So Christians joining the campaign is a form of repentance and solidarity, rather than 'I told you so.' But the fifth and last circle is a theological one. It's hope.

We approach the climate emergency with two sets of facts. One, the universe is made up of a hundred million galaxies, each of which has a hundred million stars. We're small beer. Two, the universe has existed for 14.8 billion years, humankind for 200,000 years and civilization for 6,000 or more years. We're the blink of an eye. The universe and the earth will manage just fine without us. The climate emergency is crucial not for the planet's survival, *but for ours*. Those realities should only expand our wonder at the central conviction of the Christian faith: that God chose this planet and this species with which to be in relationship, and God is invested in us, however badly we get that relationship and our relationship with the planet wrong. By investing in the planet's future, we're aligning ourselves with God's investment in it and in us. God so loved the world that we might love it too. Our hope is not that we can save the world, or that God will save us whatever happens to the world, but that God in Christ will be with us whatever happens – whatever, wherever, however, for ever.

Those are the five concentric circles of climate action. Humility, solidarity, example, accountability and hope. We can see them as the shape of Jesus' life: in Bethlehem he *humbled* himself to be born as one of us. In Nazareth he lived in *solidarity* with us for 30 years. In Galilee he set us an *example* of courage and sacrifice. On Calvary he faced the *accountability* of the distance between us and God. And at Easter, he gave us *hope* that nothing can separate us from him. All of which shows us that following Jesus, responding to the climate emergency and renewing our faith aren't rival projects. They may turn out to be the same thing.